11-12-12

One Man's Dream

My Town, My Team, My Time.

Frank White with Bill Althaus

"Frank White saved as many runs as I drove in."

Reggie Jackson
Hall of Fame slugger and member of the
500 Home Run Club

*"Frank White is the best second baseman of his generation
or any generation. He was the best. Period."*

John Schuerholz
Former Kansas City Royals general manager

*"My man Smooth helped me win a lot of games. If the ball
was hit to the right side of the infield, it was an out."*

Bret Saberhagen
Two-time Cy Young Award winner
and 1985 World Series MVP

*"We called him the Hoover, because he swept up everything
that was hit to him."*

Dan Quisenberry
Former Royals reliever and Fireman of the Year

"What made Frank so special was that he made the tough plays look easy and he made all the easy plays look easy, too."

Hal McRae
Royals designated hitter and former manager

"I called him Smooth because he was."

Darrell Porter
Royals all-star catcher

"I've seen 'em all – from Jackie (Robinson) to the second basemen who play today, and let me tell you this, Frank White was the best second baseman I ever saw. He defined the game on turf, had more range than anyone and hit cleanup in the World Series. Is Frank White a Hall of Famer? You bet he is."

Buck O'Neil
Baseball ambassador and former Negro League great

One Man's Dream

My Town, My Team,

My Time.

Frank White

with Bill Althaus

10 9 8 7 6 5 4 3 2 1

ISBN: print book 978-0-9856314-2-0
ISBN: e-book 978-0-9856314-3-7

Library of Congress Cataloging-in-Publications Data Available Upon Request

Publisher: Bob Snodgrass
Publication Coordinator: Christine Drummond
Sales and Marketing: Lenny Cohen
Editor: Blake Hughes
Dust Jacket and Book Design: Cheryl Johnson, S & Co. Design, Inc.

All photos courtesy of Frank White unless otherwise indicated.

Printed in the United States of America

www.ascendbooks.com

Chapters

Dedication:

In loving memory of my parents, Frank White Sr., and Daisie White. They taught me how to be humble and loyal, to earn respect by giving respect, and to treat others the way you would like to be treated. Thank you Mom and Dad for being great parents.

I want to thank all my children - Frank III, Adrianne, Terrance, Courtney, Michael, Darryl, Joseph and Jordan. You have done a great job keeping me young! Thank you for your love and support. I am proud to be your dad.

Also my siblings - Vernon, Mona, Joyce, Dianne, and Erna. Thanks for being there for me.

I am so humbled by the outpouring of support from my fans - I can never thank you enough. I have received support from local fans and from fans across the United States. I have a great love and appreciation for all of you.

And last, but certainly not least, my lovely wife Teresa. Without her love and support it would have been impossible to get through everything that has happened the past year. I love her so much.

1 "No, I'm serious. I want you to bat cleanup."

WHEN I WAS A KID GROWING UP IN THE INNER CITY OF KANSAS City, I remember playing baseball every day. When the sun came up, it was off to the neighborhood baseball diamond. I just made sure I had my chores done. If you couldn't find enough guys to play a game, you either improvised, or you stayed home and hit rocks with a broomstick in the driveway. I was only 7 or 8, but I'd already hit more game-winning World Series home runs than any big leaguer. My friends and I would pick the most colorful baseball names we could think of and play until our moms called us home for dinner. I was usually Diamond Jim Gentile – is that the greatest baseball name ever? The year he played for the Kansas City A's, we all wanted to be Diamond Jim. But there were other colorful names, too – Willie (Mays), The Mick (Mickey Mantle) and Johnny Callison – doesn't that just sound like the name of a baseball player? I dreamed about being a big leaguer some day, but I never dreamed about hitting cleanup in a World Series. But it happened – thanks to Dick Howser – and I knew from the moment he called me into his office and talked to me about hitting cleanup that I wasn't going to let him down.

I know I don't need to tell Kansas City Royals fans the year, because most of them will never forget that memorable 1985 season when we beat the Toronto Blue Jays in seven-game playoff series that we trailed three games to one. That let us know we could come back from any deficit and we soon found ourselves facing the same situation against the St. Louis Cardinals in the World Series. But I don't want to get too far ahead of myself. That year, the World Series didn't have a designated hitter, so Hal McRae, our designated hitter and cleanup hitter, wasn't able to make a big impact. Before the series started, I got to the ballpark for a practice and Dick Howser called me into the office and talked to me about his lineup. He said, "We can't use the DH, and since you had those 22 home runs during the season and have hit fourth a few times, I'd like you to hit cleanup."

My eyes got real big, my mouth dropped open and I know I kind of gave him that "You have to be kidding me" look. I was stunned, I couldn't believe it. I was Dick's choice to hit cleanup in a World Series that all the experts had already predicted the Cardinals would win. There was a lot of pressure on Dick, and I said, "You gotta be kidding me."

He wasn't. He just looked at me and said, "No, I'm serious. I want you to bat cleanup." When he said that, all kinds of thoughts ran through my mind. I said, "Why don't we let George (Brett) bat fourth, because I'm thinking about all the times the Cardinals will walk George in key situations if I'm not hitting well. What if we leave men on base because of me? George was used to hitting third and Dick wanted to keep him there. I was like, "Okay, I'll do it. If we do well, they can write about your good decision. If we don't, they can write about how I shouldn't have been there in the first place." I made a commitment to Dick, and he made a big commitment to me. I was not going to let him down. I'd had a pretty good power year with 22 homers, and he had confidence in me, which gave *me* confidence. I didn't want to panic. I was just wondering what the guys on the team would think.

"It was the logical choice," said McRae, who immediately threw his support to his longtime friend and teammate. "Frank was such a great second baseman that people forget how good of a hitter he became late in his career. He was a great choice to hit cleanup, and he got the job done."

No matter what happened, I was going to have fun with it. Then, I found out that only one other second baseman in all seven games of World Series history to hit cleanup was Jackie Robinson, the former Brooklyn Dodger great who broke baseball's color barrier. Just having my name mentioned in the same sentence as Jackie Robinson was inspiring and intimidating. I wasn't going to go into the Series trying to be a typical cleanup hitter – I was going to do what the situation called for. If we needed to move up a runner or lay down a bunt, I was going to do it. I wasn't going to put any extra pressure on myself, and it all worked out, but all I could see was (former Kansas City Royals manager) Whitey (Herzog, who was managing the Cardinals) walking George all the time to get to me.

Well, Game 1 rolls around and we lose 3-1. John Tudor, who was probably the best pitcher in the National League that year, shut us down. I know people looked at our lineup and thought, "What's Frank White doing hitting cleanup?" And after we lost 3-1 and didn't generate much offense, I'm sure they were asking Dick the same thing. But Dick had more confidence in me than I might have had in myself. Back in 1983 he moved me to the third spot in the order when George got hurt, and I went on to win the Player of the Year Award, so it wasn't like I was afraid I couldn't do that job. I didn't have any problems hitting fourth; I didn't have any problems facing Tudor or any of their other pitchers. I just kept thinking that this is the World Series and I've only got one shot to hit fourth and I wanted to make the most of it. I wanted to make a difference. I wanted to reward Dick for having that much confidence in me.

After that first game, reporters were asking me about hitting cleanup and about the Cardinals being such heavy favorites. I don't know why they were such heavy favorites. We had hit more home runs, I thought we were as fast as they were and even though our pitching staff was young, I thought we were as good as they were and we had (reliever Dan) Quisenberry, who was the best closer in the game.

In a short series, that first game is so important, and we had just come off that crazy series with the Blue Jays where we had to battle back from a 3-1 deficit so there wasn't any panic in our locker room. I think we were a reflection of Dick – he was calm and so were we. Dick wasn't the kind of guy to panic; he was a Yankee guy, he knew how to handle veteran guys, he knew how to handle pressure, so he didn't panic, and I think that was the most important thing for us. We'd lost the first game at home, but we knew there were six games left in the series. Once we lost Game 1, it was okay, that's gone, let's focus on game 2. Don't think too far ahead.

And then we lose Game 2, and it wasn't just that we lost it, we lost it 4-2 when St. Louis scored four runs in the top of the ninth inning. It was a well-played game and we led 2-0 going into the ninth, so it wasn't like we were getting blown out. We lost two very close games and were looking forward to taking the series to St. Louis and trying to find a way to get a win.

After we lost Game 2 at home, the mood was surprisingly upbeat. We'd been down 3-1 to Toronto so we knew we had the ability to come back in a short series. All we needed was a win – and when we landed in St. Louis, we got all the motivation we needed. When we got off the plane, we saw this large banner that said:

WELCOME TO ST. LOUIS, THE HOME OF THE 1985 WORLD SERIES CHAMPIONS.

If that doesn't motivate you, nothing will. You know that old saying, "It's never over 'til it's over." Well, that's how we felt. You could just see the mood change in all the guys when we saw that sign – and there were signs everywhere. Thank you, St. Louis, for all the motivation. And we all knew that the real motivating factor was having Sabes (Cy Young Award winner Bret Saberhagen) on the mound for Game 3. He was a skinny, young kid who was unhittable. His 1985 season was one of the best I'd ever seen. I couldn't wait for him to pitch at Busch Stadium.

I'd gone hitless in Game 1, and had three hits and an RBI in Game 2, but we lost, so I was hoping to have a breakout game in Game 3. And I did. Sabes was Sabes – he was amazing that game. We got a couple of runs in the fourth inning and we all felt like those were all the runs we'd need. Then I hit a two-run homer off (Joaquin) Andujar in the fifth, making it 4-0, and we're thinking, "Bring 'em on for Game 4." That was the longest home run I ever hit – and the most special. When I hit it, I watched (Tito) Landrum in left field and he never moved. When you're not known for hitting home runs, and you get one like that you're always going to remember it. I knew it was gone, so I wanted to make sure I ran the bases just right – not too fast and not too slow. I tried to be the ultimate professional and not show up the other team or the other pitcher. I still get chill bumps just thinking about it. I'd hit that home run a thousand times in the alley behind my house and in the park in our neighborhood, but now it really happened. I just wish I had that bat. It was one of (catcher) Jim Sundberg's bats, I shaved down the handle and it was just perfect.

Whenever I see that photo of me turning a double play against St. Louis catcher Darrell Porter, from the 1985 World Series, I get overwhelmed by the joy of bringing a world championship to Kansas City. That was our best moment as a team and my best moment as a member of the Royals because we had been unsuccessful in the 1980 World Series. None of us will ever forget 1985.

Photo courtesy of Janice Johnson.

I don't have the ball, either – but that's okay. We got the ring and that's what really matters.

That game I shared the spotlight with Sabes, who was so focused. Every time the cameras were on him in the dugout he'd pat his stomach and say hi to his wife Janeane, who was home and was about to have their first baby. He was so focused on that – but he was focused on baseball when he was out on the mound. With Sabes pitching, you knew you were going to win – and we did, 6-1. He was 20 years old and was so skinny, and he was trying to grow that little mustache of his. I bet he celebrated that night, but I was so exhausted I just went back to the hotel to rest up for the next game. There were a lot of Royals fans at the team hotel – I think it was the Clarion. It was about two blocks from the park and we walked to Busch Stadium and walked back afterwards. St. Louis was doing it up right and there were bands on every corner. There were jazz bands and blues bands and we were hoping the Cardinals would be singing the blues after Game 4.

Before Game 4, I thought a lot about our two teams. They were going for their 10th world championship. They have been around a long, long time but 10 world championships are pretty impressive. Then, I got to thinking about the Royals, and we were trying to become the first expansion team to win a World Series. We made it to the World Series in 1980, but we lost to the Phillies. They're going for a record 10th world championship, we're going for our first. This could get interesting. Well, it wasn't interesting for long. They had Tudor on the mound and he shut us out 3-0. We got another good pitching performance, but theirs was better. But after the game, the locker room was upbeat. I remember Hal was sitting in front of his locker, and his cap was sitting crazy on his head – like he always wore it – and he said, "We've got those SOBs right where we want 'em." He was referring to being down three games to one, just like we were against the Blue Jays. We had one more game in St. Louis and then it was back home to Kansas City, so we had to find a way to win Game 5.

Willie (Wilson) and I were at the park getting prepared for Game 5, and ABC was hanging the lights and stuff for the next game. They were preparing for all the postgame interviews from the locker room. I'd been in one World Series loser's locker room, and I didn't want to be in another one. If we lost Game 5 we would have had a tough time walking back to the hotel. I asked Willie what we were going to do. He turns to the guy hanging the lights and says, "You might as well take down those damn lights right now. There won't be any crying in this locker room tonight."

That was so awesome! I was so proud of Willie. I knew we were going to win the fifth game, and we did, 6-1. It was funny, both wins in St. Louis were by the same score, 6-1. Sabes pitched real well and Danny Jackson matched him pitch for pitch in the fifth game. Charlie (Leibrandt) and Buddy (Black) had each pitched well enough to win, but Sabes and D.J. just rose to the occasion and made sure the series returned back to Kansas City. The plane ride home after Game 5 was business as usual. I wish we could have taken a riverboat home or taken a train and stopped at all the little towns along the way. I heard about the dorm rooms at MU where one side was all Cardinals and the other side was all Royals. The entire state was so excited about this series and so was I. We were down three games to two and knew we were going to win the next two games – we just knew it. Charlie was pitching Game 6 and we had a lot of confidence in him. I was thinking about being a little kid, hitting rocks with a broomstick, dreaming about the World Series, and I was flying home for Game 6. Does life get any more exciting than this?

"My dad had never been in the clubhouse. My entire family was there. And it was just unbelievable."

Game 6 – do or die. We wanted our city to be able to experience what St. Louis had experienced nine times – being a championship city. It's usually Game 7 that everyone remembers from a World Series, but for us, it was Game 6. For one day, people forgot about their problems, and they watched their team try to reach the goal of winning a championship. People in St. Louis were used to it – people in Kansas City wanted to experience it for the first time.

I had a hard time sleeping before Game 6. There was a lot of anxiety, a lot of excitement and a lot of nervous tension. And we just soaked it all in. None of us believed it would be our last game and we got all fired up when we saw all the champagne being taken into the Cardinals locker room.

Everyone talks about the plays in the bottom of the ninth, but one mistake earlier in the game might have changed the outcome and made Don Denkinger's life a lot easier. I was on first base and stole second. I was clearly safe, but was called out. Pat Sheridan followed with a single that should have given us a 1-0 lead. Instead, Brian Harper singles home Terry Pendleton with the Cardinals' only run in the top of the ninth inning, and we're down to our final three outs.

Whitey brought in Todd Worrell, their closer, and the first batter he faced was Jorge Orta. Jorge hit a ground ball to Jack Clark at first. Worrell was covering first and had the ball before Jorge reached the base, but Denkinger called him safe. Needless to say, that caused a lot more commotion than the missed call on me earlier in the game. Whitey was really upset, but the ruling stood and Steve Balboni came up. He hit a high pop up near first base and it fell between Clark and (catcher Darrell) Porter. Balboni then singled and Onix Concepcion went in as a pinch runner. Jim Sundberg attempted a sacrifice bunt, but Worrell fielded it and forced Jorge at third base.

We had runners on first and second and Porter had a passed ball, so we had runners on second and third. They walked Hal (McRae) to load the bases with one out. Dick sent in Dane Iorg, a former Cardinal to pinch hit, and he hit a soft liner into right field. Andy Van Slyke, who had one of the strongest arms in the National League, threw a perfect throw home but Sunny slid around Porter's tag and we won 2-1.

I was able to see Sunny slide around Porter's tag, but that was all I saw that inning because I was up in the manager's office with (ABC commentator and Hall of Fame slugger) Reggie Jackson.

At the start of the inning, I went into the clubhouse. Reggie was doing the game for ABC and he was in Dick's office, so I went in and watched the game on TV. After being called out at second base on a bad call earlier in the game, there was no way I was going to sit in the dugout and watch the Cardinals celebrate a championship in my town. I was PO'd. I'm in the clubhouse just walking around in circles, when Reggie sees me. There's the Denkinger play, the dropped foul ball, Balboni's hit, and I'm ready to go back to the dugout. But Reggie grabs my arm and says, "No, no, no – you can't leave. You can't go out there." He's holding onto me real tight and I can't go. And then we try to bunt Orta and he gets forced at third. Then the passed ball! I'm really trying to go now and Reggie says, you can't leave, you can't leave. Then they walk the bases loaded, and I say, "I gotta get the hell out there."

He's still holding my arm when Iorg gets the hit. I'm running out of Dick's office, flying down the tunnel, and it was so exciting. If Iorg would have hit the ball harder, Van Slyke would have probably thrown Sunny out at the plate. But Sunny made this great slide around Darrell Porter and (shortstop) Buddy (Biancalana) was jumping around and everyone is going crazy. That was my single greatest moment as a Royal. When we scored that run, we all knew we were going to win

There are pictures that are worth a thousand words, and this is one of them. George had just caught the ball to record the last out of Game 3 of the 1985 American League Championship Series. We were down two games to none, and eventually would be down 3-1 before coming back to beat the Blue Jays in the seventh and deciding game. He shows me the ball after that final out and we know we're heading in the right direction.

(AP Photo/Paul Wagner)

Game 7. We all celebrated, and someone in the dog pile accidently hit (pitcher) Mike Jones in the nose and broke it. He's bleeding all over everyone and we just kept celebrating. When we got back to the tunnel leading to the locker room, it was almost like everybody poured in through the clubhouse doors at the same time the players came in. I mean we had wives and kids and everybody. The clubhouse kids were scrambling to remove some questionable posters and material the guys might not have wanted their wives or girlfriends to see – but it was crazy. You never forget a moment like that. It was like we had won it all – and it was just Game 6. My dad had never been in the clubhouse, and they were all there. The players were chanting. "We Want Tudor!" You could just feel the momentum swing. It was unbelievable – I had never felt emotion like that in our locker room. Here we are, on the biggest stage in baseball, and we're ready for Game 7 – I mean, we're really ready. We'd have played it that night if they would have let us.

"Dick, this one's for you. Thanks for the opportunity and the confidence."

I have to be honest with you. Did we really need to play Game 7 after what had happened the night before? I have never been in a more confident clubhouse than ours the night before Game 7 and the hours before we played that final game. We knew it was going to be a different game. We didn't think they could come back from Game 6, and we had Sabes on the mound. That's an unbeatable combination. They were throwing Tudor, who had two wins against us, but he wasn't the same pitcher in Game 7. We got five runs in just over two innings. They used seven pitchers and we hit every one of them. Darryl Motley hit a big homer for us early in this game. We all knew this game was going to be different and it was. Motley hit a long foul ball that looked like it was going to be a homer, and he cracked his bat. He came up to the plate with a new bat and hit a home run in almost the same spot. I got on base and scored a run later in the game and we're all thinking, "Let's get this over so we can start celebrating." Darryl got us going early on with the homer and he caught the last out in right field. He started jumping, I started jumping – we were all jumping. The cover of *Sports*

Illustrated the next week showed all the guys celebrating, but I wasn't in the picture because I was out waiting to congratulate Darryl and the other outfielders. I started thinking about the guys on the team who were the unsung heroes – guys like Lynn Jones, Pat Sheridan, Greg Pryor and Dane Iorg, getting Lonnie Smith in a trade, and how Sunny (Sundberg) handled the young pitchers.

That was the year (general manager John) Schuerholz made all the right moves. Everything fell into place – the great young pitchers, the veterans we had – Willie and George had great years. That's how you win a championship. People asked me if I talked to Whitey during the series, and I didn't. I never really talked to my managers. I asked them what they wanted from me before the start of the season and I told themI would give them everything I had. I just felt the best thing a manager could do for me was put my name in the lineup. As long as they did that, whatever happened was on me. You know, I didn't care who the manager was, cause I figured a manager isn't a bad manager as long as he puts my name in the lineup. Whitey gave me a chance to become an all-around player, and I appreciate that. He took the hand-cuffs off and let me play. I didn't need to look over my shoulder with Whitey, because if I did my job, he left me alone and let me play. But it was Dick who saw something in me that no other manager saw. He saw a lot more.

Winning that first playoff game against the Blue Jays was special because we had swept the Yankees in 1980 when Dick was their manager and it cost him his job. Now, five years later, he's our manager and we win the World Series. He was a players' manager and we all loved playing for him. Looking back on it all, it was like, "Dick, this one's for you. Thanks for the opportunity and the confidence." One of my lasting memories of that World Series was Dick coming onto the field after we won, tucking his lucky hat into his jacket. Every guy on the team would tell you that we wanted to get that World Series for Dick, and we did."

I didn't have much to talk about following my first World Series. We lost to Philadelphia in six games and I think I had two hits. After a series like that, you want to redeem yourself. I led the World Series with six RBIs against the Cardinals and had the home run in our first win at St. Louis. I was so tired of reading in the paper and watching on TV how the Royals had no chance to win that series. We didn't get the job done in 1980, but we got a second chance and took care of business in 1985 – and we did it against our cross-state rivals. For a kid who hit all those World Series homers in the alley behind his house in downtown Kansas City, it was the perfect ending to a perfect season.

This is a John Martin poster the Kansas City Royals distributed during the 10th anniversary of our 1985 World Series triumph over the St. Louis Cardinals. From upper left, Dane Iorg, who hit the dramatic game-winning single in Game 6; Bret Saberhagen, the World Series MVP; George Brett, the Hall of Fame third baseman who always came up with the big hit; me, hitting my World Series home run; Mr. and Mrs. Kauffman, who really deserved to be the owners of a world championship team; and Jim Sundberg, whose game-winning slide in Game 6 helped us live to play another day. I could look at that painting all day and never get tired of it. Courtesy of John Martin.

2 "They had a small house, but they had the best outside toilet in Grapeland."

MY FATHER, FRANK WHITE, SR., WAS BORN IN GREENVILLE, Mississippi, and that's where my brother, two older sisters and I grew up. We moved to Kansas City when I was 5 or 6 and my two younger sisters were born here. And oh, my goodness, were we ever glad to move up to Missouri, because that meant no more picking cotton. Well, that's not entirely right, because my mom and dad would send us back down to Grapeland, Mississippi in the summer to live with my grandparents, Roosevelt and Bertha Mitchell. Oh, did we pick cotton. They were sharecroppers and had a small wood house with a tin roof. When it rained, it was so loud. When the rain hit, it sounded like gravel was being dumped on top of you. It's funny the little things you remember when you were a kid, but I will always remember how it sounded when rain hit Grandma and Grandpa Mitchell's house. They would catch rain water in a 35-gallon barrel and use it to wash their hair. They had a small house, but they had the best outside toilet in Grapeland. Everyone else had a one seater, but Grandma and Grandpa had a two seater. Everyone around used to make a big deal out of it but I just kept wondering why two people would want to be sitting next to each other in that hot box at the same time? But Grandma and Grandpa had it all figured out. If one of the kids had to use the bathroom in the middle of the night, they had a large basin for No. 1 and gave you a flashlight for No. 2. You had to walk past the chicken coop and the hog pen – and there was no telling what you were going to step on – or step in – on your way to the two seater. See why all the kids were so happy to have moved to Kansas City? But we loved visiting our grandparents. They made sure we worked so hard during the day that we didn't get into any trouble at night. And my mom, Daisie, knew that I loved to eat bread. I used to cry for it at night, so she would always put a piece of bread under my pillow so I would wake up and find it – and my grandma did the same thing. When I think back, my mom and dad raised six kids, none of us wound up in jail or doing drugs and they had a plan for all of us and we turned out all right.

My mom had a sister named Louella Bradley. She moved up to Kansas City from down south, and I think she must have talked so much about it that everybody just sort of followed her. It was like a migration from the south, to come north and find better jobs and better living conditions.

"You didn't trust walking the highways at night. You'd see a car coming and you'd jump in a ditch until it passed you by."

Mississippi was the poorest state in the Union back when I was growing up, and sometimes, I think a poor attitude goes right along with that. It was tough being black anywhere in the United States back

then, but it was really tough in Mississippi. You didn't trust the highways at night. You'd see a car coming and you'd jump in a ditch until is passed you by. Or you'd go the back way through the cemetery so people wouldn't see you – we did that a lot. We're talking the 1950s and '60s and down there, you knew how people felt. They wore their feelings on

Who's that handsome young guy? That is my sophomore photo from Lincoln High School. That seems like such a long, long time ago.

24

their sleeves, but I could deal with that. When we moved north, people disguised their feelings so you didn't always know where they were coming from. I won't say life was horrible, but it's a lot better today. My grandparents were great, and everybody worked hard. You know they had the normal things a farm had – a mule, pigs and chickens. They had about 20 acres, and I believe they were sharecroppers. There was a cemetery behind the house and all kinds of pecan trees. We had all the things you needed to survive. We made our own ice cream and butter – we ate good – but we needed to eat because we worked so hard picking all that cotton. That was the worst, the absolute worst.

It was so hot down there, so we'd get up early and do our chores. One day we might have to feed the pigs. Another day we might collect eggs. We'd get all our chores done early and then go to summer school until noon. When we got home, Grandma had a big lunch; then we went off to the fields. We'd pick cotton until it got dark. Sometimes when we went out at night we had to be careful and dive down in that ditch if we saw a car coming. Nothing ever happened, probably because we were so aware of everything going on around us.

Our ditch-jumping days ended when we moved to Kansas City. We were a lucky group of kids to have such wonderful parents. Both my parents were very humble. My mom went to church every Sunday, and made sure we had the best we could have – nice clothes, things like that. They both instilled a good work ethic, and back then both your parents worked. Mom worked in the garment industry all her life down on 9th and Central, pressing clothes. When my dad left the cotton fields in Mississippi, he came here and worked various jobs with different car dealers, from porter to cleanup guy. He hooked up with Art Bunker Volkswagen on 79th and Wornall, until he retired. He was a real likeable guy who fished all the time.

My dad showed me everything a dad should teach a son – how to treat women, how to change tires, points and plugs on a car, how to hunt and fish, but baseball wise he never missed a game – he was asked to leave some of them – but he was always there when they started. When I was playing a position he was fine, but when I pitched he didn't always see eye to eye with the umpire, so he watched a few games from the car.

I learned so much from my dad, but the biggest lesson he taught me was respect. He said that whatever I did, to be passionate about it, to enjoy it, to have fun with it. He just enjoyed watching me play or doing whatever I did with him, whereas my mom enjoyed getting trophies. I remember when I was 12 and I gave her a football trophy and she put it on the mantle. I never did get a baseball trophy, even though I was playing on the best team in the league. After the third game, my dad was wondering what was going on, because I never played. Before the game was over, he took me off the bench and took me home. I was embarrassed and was wondering what was going on. We got home and I asked him why he took me off the team.

He asked me, "Do you love baseball?" and I told him I did. So he asked me, "Are you learning how to play the game?" And I told him I was learning – and that's when he looked at me and said, "You're not learning by sitting on the bench." He believed the only way you could learn the game was by being out on the field. I don't think I agreed with him at the time, but looking back at it, I know what he was talking about. You can't sit on the bench while everyone else is playing and consider that playing baseball. And back then, we didn't know how good I was going to be, but he knew that I wasn't going to be very good unless I was out there playing the game. So he put me on the worst team in the league and guess what? I played every day, I learned about the game, got better and better, and I learned a valuable life lesson that I remember to this day.

He also taught me something else – something that might be even more important than the aspects of the game. He told me, "I want you to be good at what you do. I want you to enjoy what you do, but you want people to like you for what you do. But I want you to be humble and never show off or boast about what you do." I'm sure that's a big reason I always enjoyed being around the fans, getting to know them and letting them get to know me. When I played, I always gave the other guy credit, and I made sure my teammates got credit and that we talked about the team approach. If I can say anything about what my dad taught me, he taught me about having the right approach to the game and to life. That's where my temperament came from."

That lesson in life is evident more than 48 years after Frank White Sr., taught his son the importance of treating people with respect.

"Who are you?" asked the lady in the downtown parking garage toll booth.

"I'm Frank White, ma'am," Frank replied, with a smile.

The digital thermometer listed the temperature at 103 degrees and Frank and his wife Teresa had discussed the possibility of how long it would take to fry an egg on the sidewalk outside of City Hall, where Frank had just been recognized by the Mayor for being Kansas City's ambassador during the All-Star Game that was played in Kauffman Stadium. All he wanted to do was get back home to Lee's Summit where he could unwind and get into some air conditioning.

"I knew that was you," the elderly lady said, throwing her hands into the air. "Frank White! You were my favorite player. God bless you Frank White!"

Frank simply smiled and thanked the garage employee for remembering him. As she punched his ticket and gave him change for his payment, he looked at his wife Teresa and smiled.

He didn't say it – but you knew he was thinking, "That's why this is my town."

I played 18 years with the Royals and never got kicked out of a game – and I think I owe that to my dad, too. I know a lot of people are surprised by that, but I always felt like you were being paid to play and not to get yourself kicked out, so I kept my emotions in check and played the game the way it should be played. If you get kicked out, you are replaced by someone who might not be at your skill level, you let the team down, you let your fans down, and I would have felt like I let my dad down, too. I think my dad was proud that I never got kicked out, and looking back on it, I'm proud of it, too.

Now, things were a little bit different when I was managing in the minors. I got kicked out of a few games, but sometimes it was your players who got you kicked out. There are different reasons managers get kicked out, because there is a fine line as to just how far you can go. I tried to never step over that line, but sometimes, you just can't help yourself.

"You know, we had white only bathrooms and drinking fountains, and stuff like that."

When I was going down to my grandparents, I was probably 5 or 6. I think I was maybe 10 or 11 when I first realized that things were different between whites and blacks. I wasn't sure why it was happening, but I knew it was happening. You know, we had white only bathrooms and drinking fountains, and stuff like that. And we just accepted it. It was the way it was, and that was pretty much it. We weren't going to change it, and we didn't have to like it, but we accepted it. My parents told us about segregation and we faced it everywhere we lived. Like I was saying earlier, it was much more evident in the deep south. When we went to school, there were just black kids in the school. And it was segregated in Kansas City to a degree. When we first came up here we lived with my Aunt Louella for a couple of years over at 2805 Highland. We lived in her basement, and we had it all sectioned off, so we could be to ourselves. And then in 1959, I believe, we moved to 29th and Olive and never moved again. We lived downtown, and there were diner counters where blacks weren't allowed to eat. Kansas City had its problems, every place had its problems. But my mom and dad took good care of us – real good care. I think for the most part my dad was mild-mannered, but he had that edge about him. You know, he still was from the South and he hated to be taken advantage of. He would fight if he was pushed into a corner, but most of the time he would just get into a routine and go hunting and fishing and be there for his family and work. He supported everything his kids did, and he was the same with his grandkids and great grandkids.

When I reflect on my life, there are some special moments. I'll never forget getting my first baseball glove. It was a first baseman's mitt. I played first back then and I loved that glove, even though it was more plastic than leather. The worst thing that you could do was leave it out in the rain. I also loved westerns, and I remember one Christmas I got a cap gun and holster. Then, when I was older I got a

BB gun and a Western Flyer wagon. But my biggest gift was a bicycle. I think I was in second grade, and I loved that bike. I was riding in the neighborhood and a kid asked me if he could ride it. He took off – and never came back. I was crushed and I knew my dad was going to kill me. I was worried all day about what he was going to say. I was in the front yard when I saw him driving down the street, holding my bike on the top of his car. I ran out and asked him where he found it and he said, "I saw this kid riding your bike. I knew it wasn't his, so I got it back for you." I don't know if I was ever more relieved in my life. I loved him to death, but I was nervous about what he might say. My dad was in World War II, so even when we went to the World Series, he never would fly. He said, "My last flight was from Germany to the States." He wouldn't get on another plane, so he missed the games in Philadelphia and St. Louis.

He was a man of routines. He would hunt and fish, and when he came to our Royals games, he would come with his buddies. Early in my career I left him some tickets and a guy sitting behind him spilled beer down his back, and he told me, "If that happens a lot, I'm

There's a chapter in the book where I talk about finally getting a baseball trophy for mother, and this is the team that won the championship. This is a 14-year-old Hallmark Card team that won the Connie Mack League championship. I'm the second player from the left on the front row and that trophy and big smile were for my mom.

going to be fighting a lot." So he and his friends stood on the rail and watched the game from there while my mom would sit in her seat behind home plate. They would lean on the railing, and wore all the finish off the rails, so the Royals padded the rails for my dad and his Rail Boys, and no one had more fun at games than my dad and his friends. And they would bet on everything – who was going to get the first hit, who was going to strike out first. He was into the game. He loved it almost as much as I did. He played some amateur baseball, and I think one day my mom gave him an ultimatum. You know - me or baseball. And he always regretted not continuing. The Negro Leagues were just winding down and I think he had a shot at going down and playing with the Memphis Red Sox. My mom said she would not go with him, and that was the end of his baseball career. Looking back on it, I can only imagine how tough that was for him. When I was asked to go to the Royals Academy, my son Frank was a baby. I could go to Florida and play for $50 a month or stay here and make $100 a week working as a shipping clerk at Metals Protection Plating Company. And I think if my first wife, Gladys would have said it's "me or the highway," I would have stayed home. So I think support is what any person needs. Everybody's got their own selfish reasons for why they do things, but I think if you are really, truly partners in the whole deal you're going to support one another regardless of the outcome. So Gladys and our son Frank moved in with my mom and dad. Mr. Kauffman got Gladys a job working in the Royals ticket office at the stadium. My mom and dad would watch Frank, and they really enjoyed being around Gladys. It's was like "Big Mama's House," (the Martin Lawrence comedy). There were kids and family members everywhere, and everyone always seemed to be enjoying themselves. Our home was the place everybody migrated to. It was the house in the neighborhood that always had something going on – it wasn't a house, it was a home. That's how it was for as long as I can remember. And my mom loved it. Daisie was quiet, but she was feisty. She was stern, she laughed a lot, she went to Morning Star Baptist Church every Sunday and when she told you to do something, if you didn't move fast enough, then something was going to come flying in your direction.

2

She worked hard every day of her life, and she was a fighter. You had to be, back in the day, and I think we – my brother and sisters – saw how hard my parents worked and how much they loved us, and that instilled a strong work ethic in each one of us. If your parents aren't afraid to work, you shouldn't be afraid to work. There wasn't any sitting around at our home. After I graduated from Lincoln High School, I was sitting at home and my dad asked me what I was going to do. I said, I didn't know. He said, "Milk and bread cost a lot!" So I started looking for a job, and got one as a stock handler at Hallmark Cards. I was making $100 a week. I paid my parents $100 a month rent and it made me feel good. I was dating Gladys at the time, but I didn't have the responsibilities that would come with a wife and child. I was one of the lucky kids in the neighborhood because I had two parents and there was a lot of love in our house.

I knew so many kids from broken homes, kids who just walked the streets – and if they weren't looking for trouble, it usually found them. If they couldn't get along with their parents, they wound up on a couch or in a sleeping bag on the floor of our house. My mom and dad would never turn away any kid, especially if they were family or friends. We were the lucky ones. I think that even back then I realized how important and special it was to have two parents. They had to work, so my older brother Vernon and I would go through a routine every morning. We'd get our sisters ready for the babysitter or school, we'd comb and braid their hair, we'd iron our clothes, do all the chores that needed to be done and then get off to school ourselves. We had a calendar and we'd write which chores we needed to do, and we knew that they better be done before mom and dad got home. We knew who was going to wash our clothes and who was going to wash the dishes; we had a system, and that system worked. And we knew that where we lived wasn't the safest part of Kansas City, so we took care of our sisters and we survived. Yeah, we survived.

Back then there was probably a little gang on every corner. We lived on 29th Street, so from, 31st Street to 27th Street, and 25th Street all the way down to Truman Road, there was always something to deal with. But we knew there was safety in numbers, so we made sure to stay together as a family or always tried to be with our friends. I didn't like fighting, but if I had to, I would. And if a bully knew you were willing to fight, he would usually leave you alone and go pick on someone else. But there were always the older guys who would just stand on street corners and take your milk money. We knew who they were and what corners they were standing on. It was as if the young kids were salmon swimming upstream and the older kids were the grizzlies swatting us out of the water. It was pretty easy pickings for them, so you had to avoid them at any cost. If you needed to walk a few blocks out of your way to get to school or get home you did it. That's what I mean when I talk about survival. You find a way to survive.

I wasn't a perfect kid growing up, but I never got into any serious trouble. I knew kids who were doing drugs, hanging out with the wrong people, in their own little gangs – but I wasn't interested in that stuff. You could be going somewhere and before you knew it, you were in the middle of something you didn't want to be associated with. So I made sure to hang around with my friends and avoid situations like that. What helped me a lot was my dad started taking me hunting at an early age. And I was always playing baseball, so I didn't have the time to get in trouble. While guys were drinking and hanging out on the corner, I was playing ball or hunting. When it came to parties and being around girls, I was a little bit slow. I just didn't care about that kind of stuff. I had my friends, we hung out and I stayed away from trouble. However, I do remember one fight I got in in seventh grade. I don't even remember what it was about. My older sister Mona was the fighter in the family. She was a tomboy and would just as soon fight a boy as a girl. Well, this kid down the block was giving her a hard time, so I fought him, and I think I won. My dad came home that night and said that he had heard I'd been in a fight. He asked me who won, and I told him that I really didn't know. So he takes me back to the kid's house and makes us fight again. I actually won that one, and I was mad and confused. When my dad took me back home, he said, that if you fight, you need to have a winner - because if there's no winner, you're just going to keep fighting. You'll fight tomorrow and you'll fight the next day, and the next. And he was right. That kid and I never fought again.

Thinking back to those days really does stir up some memories. My home was *my home*, the neighborhood was *my neighborhood*, and nothing really ever changed. Even when I signed to play with the Royals and got called up to the big leagues, I was still just the kid from the neighborhood. People were excited and happy for me, but there weren't any parties or balloons or anything like that. I still lived at home, cut the grass, visited with the neighbors and saw my friends. It wasn't like everyone would be waiting for me to get home after a game because I was playing for the Royals. They were all happy for me. At the stadium it was a big deal. My dad would be up on the rail with his

I wish I had that body back! One of the greatest things about writing this book was being able to look back on my on-field career and all the great highlights. I loved playing for the Royals, and no one can ever take that away from me.

friends, and my mom would be sitting in her seat with her friend Linda Scroggins or one of my brothers or sisters. Linda was a super fan who became good friends with my mom. Mom and dad came to as many games as they could, but when my dad passed away Oct. 24, 2004, a lot of things changed. One thing that was very special to me was that the Royals unveiled my statue in August of 2004, so my mom and dad were both there to see that. But he was gone a few months later.

My dad had two boats and a truck. They were just sitting in the yard, so my friend, Ron Hilliard, and I redid one boat, sold it and gave mom the money, and we donated the other boat to charity. I'd go over and drive the truck, just so it wouldn't sit in the yard all day. I made a real conscious effort to be around her a lot. I looked a lot like my dad and I thought that by seeing me, it would help remind her of him, and that would help. We painted the inside of her house bright yellow and she really liked that. And I went by and saw her every day, and I know she liked that a lot. When I had to go to spring training with the team, I called her every night. You could tell she was coming out of her depression and that was good. It made me feel a lot better. We had one conversation a long time after my dad passed and she told me the one thing she regretted was not going back to church after he passed away. I don't know whether it was because his funeral was at her church and all the memories it brought back – she never did say – but you could tell that it left a big void in her life. She still sent the church money every week and that was important to her. My dad never went to church because he was always hunting or fishing, and I never heard her talk to him about why he didn't go. Later in his life, he would make a conscious effort to be home and be around his family on Sundays. So one day I asked him, "How come you never go to church." He said, "I don't need to go to church to know where I'm going." He was like that. He had all these sayings. One day I was in a slump. We were talking and he said, "Son, the sun don't shine on the same dog's ass every day." I just said, "Okay, thanks." Mom's favorite saying was, "What's done in the dark will soon come to light." They were always coming up with stuff like that. They were so different in so many ways, but then again, they were a lot alike.

When my mom quit coming to games, she began listening to them on the radio or watching on TV with my brother Vernon. When I began broadcasting, they would critique my ties. After the games, I would call her and we'd talk about my ties, or the game, or anything she wanted to talk about. She would stay up late and I knew she would be sitting by her phone, waiting for me to call. We had our routine of talking every day until she passed in February of 2010.

3 "I remember lying on the floor, hearing the police sirens and gunfire off in the distance. It was a scary time."

I GREW UP IN A VERY POLITICALLY CHARGED TIME. WHEN WE FIRST moved up here from Mississippi, I went to Wendall Phillips Elementary School, and in the fourth grade I went to Linwood Elementary. That's where I had my first experience with busing. I didn't like it, and I didn't understand it. I took a bus to the west side of town. I never had any problem with the kids, but I had some problems with the teachers. They always wanted to spank you, and back then they could. It wasn't like it is today – they were paddle happy – and I was a good kid and a good student. But that wasn't nearly as bad as the fear I had down in Mississippi where I jumped in ditches to keep from being seen by cars at night.

For a while, that lingering fear was a distant memory. But it returned in Kansas City in 1968. It was the year Martin Luther King was assassinated, and we had riots in our neighborhood. I remember lying on the floor, hearing the police sirens and gunfire off in the distance. It was a scary time. The police were being attacked in certain areas right near our house, and every time we went outside the police would yell at us to show them our hands – they wanted to make sure we weren't carrying any weapons such as guns or knives, you know, anything that could do some damage in a riot situation. I was a senior in high school and I wasn't a political kid, but it had an impact – a big impact.

The worst riot was only two blocks from where we lived. My sister Mona was pregnant and went into labor, and my dad had to get her to the hospital. That's my dad – he goes through a riot, gunfire, all that stuff – to get his little girl to the hospital. You had to have a special pass just to be out driving because the police wanted to make sure you weren't out trying to do any harm to anyone. Everything turned out fine; none of my family was involved in any of the destruction, our home survived, but there were some mental issues we all had to deal with. Just look back, 1968 was a different year. It was the era of radical politics, Bobby Kennedy, Martin Luther King, Malcom X, the Vietnam War. The Black Panthers were on the rise and it was something you had to address with your family and your friends. There weren't counselors at school that I remember; it was a tougher time and you had to figure things out for yourself. I talked a lot to my parents, my grandparents, my brother and sisters, and we got through it. Unfortunately, some kids and some families didn't. That's why my family has always been so important to me. Two great parents, two wonderful grandparents – we didn't have much, but we had a lot of love in our house.

Love and a lot of smarts. We knew what we could, and couldn't do. I went to Lincoln High School at 22nd and Brooklyn – where Municipal Stadium used to be. Right there on the corner. Like we talked about before, there was a gang on every corner – you had gangs on 25th and Brooklyn, 27th and Brooklyn, and 31st and Brooklyn, so you had to weave through that stuff every day.

I remember seeing my first gang fight. I wasn't in it – I was just watching, and I was scared. It was a bunch of guys from our neighborhood, and you just hoped no one pulled out a gun or a knife. Switchblades were big back then – they might still be – and I just kept thinking, "Don't go pulling no gun or knife." It's hard to explain; gang fights would just kind of spring up – they just happened, they were a part of my life – a part I'd like to forget.

It helped that I played sports. They knew who I was and sometimes that helped, sometimes it didn't. I never started a fight, but I never walked away from one if I felt threatened. By threatened, I mean threatened to fight. I wasn't going to get involved in anything with guns or knives because I had too many friends who were killed doing that kind of stuff. They were friends when we were young, but they just got into bad stuff when they got older. A lot of it involved drugs and girls. I wasn't involved in drugs – never was, no way – and I wasn't going to get shot over a girl. You had to be smart, because you could wind up dead if you were stupid in the inner city.

3

Back then, if you were going to fight, you did it in the parking lot of a movie theater in the neighborhood. Everyone was there, everyone knew what was going on – it was a fist fight. When it was over, it was over. Today, I tell my kids, you can get shot if you honk at someone for cutting you off in the parking lot.

"Spring Valley Park was my second home."

I remember talking to (late Hall of Fame outfielder) Kirby Puckett one time, and he told me that the projects in Chicago where he grew up didn't have any place to play baseball. He told me he didn't even know what grass looked like until he got out of the projects. But that didn't stop him from playing ball or loving life. He was such a special guy – always smiling, always happy, always so enthusiastic. When he was a kid, there wasn't anyone to play with, so he would play catch with his mom or he would just throw a ball against a wall – and he'd do it for hours. I was always disappointed that we didn't have baseball at Lincoln High School, but at least we had a park that we could walk to every day. Spring Valley Park was my second home. It was two blocks west of Olive on Brooklyn and it had two baseball diamonds. We didn't have a lot of organized baseball, so a bunch of us kids would just go down there and play all day. We didn't have coaches, we didn't need them. All we wanted to do was play. I first started playing organized ball when I was 9. I had my plastic glove and I played with it until I was a lot older. Then I got a leather glove, but it wasn't fancy or anything like that. My dad probably got it at a thrift store. It didn't have any player's name on it, it was just a glove. But it was my glove and I took care of it. The older I got, the better I got. And I played for some pretty good teams. When I was 18, I played for Safeway, and my coach, Hilton Smith, was a great Negro League pitcher who is in the Major League Baseball Hall of Fame. He had a great curve ball and we talked a lot about pitching. I was a pretty good pitcher back then. There was another kid, Benny Vann, and he played with Friendship Baptist. He was a lefty, and I was a righty, and when we pitched, there were a lot of people watching. All the guys would be in the park playing dominoes, and when the lights went on at the park, they packed up their dominoes and came over and watched the game. There was a real buzz, the stands were full and it was a lot of fun. Those are the things I like to remember about my teenage years – not the bad stuff – the good stuff, the fun stuff. And the fun was just about to begin because it wasn't long before I tried out for the Royals Academy and my life would change forever.

4 "You need to take a chance on this kid."

I ALWAYS WANTED TO PLAY BASEBALL, BUT I NEVER THOUGHT I COULD play and get paid for it. I dreamed about it, but you dream about a lot of things that never happen. I knew my mom and dad worked hard, and I wanted to work hard, too. But if I could work hard and play baseball, that would be the perfect situation. Baseball was always a game to me. Even when I was getting paid to play, it was still a game, and it was a game I loved. I didn't think about the financial aspects, I was just a kid. But I had to start thinking about things like that. In high school, I was a skinny kid who weighed 130 pounds as a freshman. But my senior year, I went from about 145 pounds to 170 pounds and I looked like an athlete. I was one of the kids in the inner city that people knew about. I was working for Metals Protection plating company on Truman Road, and I thought I might work there the rest of my life. I was making good money, and I was still playing baseball. There was all this talk about the Royals holding a tryout for this new baseball academy. It was the dream of Ewing Kauffman, the team owner, to have an academy where the Royals could develop their own players. I kind of heard about it, but I didn't think much about it because I was working and didn't think I'd be able to get off work to tryout.

Then Coach Smith and Bill Rowan, my high school science teacher and basketball coach, talked to me and they said I should try out. And I also talked with Scout Bob Thurman, Don Motley and his brother Bob, the last living umpire from the Negro Leagues.

"I told Frank to go to the tryouts and make us proud," said Don Motley, who is involved with the Negro League Baseball Museum. "Frank was special, you could tell it the first time you saw him. Now, we didn't think that one day he'd have a statue at the stadium and be in the Royals Hall of Fame, but we knew he had great potential. And we were right."

I asked my boss, Herbert Bozart, for a couple of days off and he wanted to know why I was asking. I told him I wanted to try out for this baseball academy the Royals were starting and he gave me the days off. I owe him a lot for that. My life would be a lot different if he would have said no. So I go down to Municipal Stadium at 9 a.m. and there are like 300 guys out on the field. I thought, "What have I gotten myself into?" I found out that it was a two-day tryout. We ran a 60-yard dash, they watched us throw and take ground balls and they took us down under the stadium to see Dr. Riley – I called him the Mind Doctor – and he did all these things involving coordination. He played with your head a little bit. He'd give you a deck of cards and have you match all the suits as fast as you could. I kind of thought they were interested in me, because they didn't take all the guys down to see the Mind Doctor. Later, I went to the batting cage and (Kansas City A's first baseman) Norm Siebern was there by the cage. I saw him talking with someone and heard him say, "You need to take a chance on this kid." And he was talking about me. They were talking about how old I was, and Siebern said it didn't matter, that I was an athlete. Then I heard something that broke my heart; they weren't going to take any married players down to the academy and I was married and had a son. So, when I left, I thought that was it. It was back to the plating company and my baseball days were coming to an end.

Then, something that only happens in movies happened to me. Later that day, I was at my parents' house and I hear this commotion outside. I look out the window and there is a big blue limo parked in front of our house. The driver is a big, well-dressed black man. He gets out of the car and comes up and knocks on the door. I go to the door and he says, "Mr. Kauffman would like to speak with you." I look out and don't see Mr. K in the limo, so I ask Blanchie Blevens– the limo driver – if he is going to take me to meet Mr. K. And he tells me Mr. K is waiting to talk with me on the phone in his limo. I know everyone in the neighborhood is wondering what the hell is going on, and I'm wondering that, too. So Blanchie takes me out to the limo, and there is this box thing with a phone attached. He takes the phone off the receiver, hands it to me, and I hear Mr. K say, "Frank, this is Ewing Kauffman." I'd never talked on a phone in a car before – I didn't even know there was anything like that – and we started our conversation. He told me that he heard a lot of good things about me and he wanted me to go to his academy. I asked him how much I would be making and he said $50, plus room and board. After taxes, I was going to make $48 a month, and I was making $100 a week at my job, so I told him I would have to think about it. Mr. K was a smart, smart man and he knew what he was doing. He told me that a catcher named Art Sanchez, who was also married, was going to the academy and he told me that he would give my wife Gladys a job at the stadium in the ticket office. You hear about the money guys make today when they are drafted right out of college or high school, and I was a month away from my 20th birthday, with a wife and son and was being offered $48 a month to live my dream. We talked a little bit more and I thanked him and told him I had to talk to Gladys and my parents. I told him that I would get back in touch with him. I handed the phone to Blanchie, and I looked around the neighborhood at everyone watching me and wondered what had just happened. I talked with Gladys and my parents, and they said Gladys and Frank could move in with them. I got back to Mr. K, and said yes.

> "The only mandatory course that Mr. K made us take was public speaking, because he thought that would be something we'd need once we got into Major League Baseball."

I remember I had trouble sleeping that night. It was June and I was leaving for the academy in early August. I'd dreamed about being a big leaguer and I was a step closer. I thought about PeeWee Reese and Dizzy Dean, who used to broadcast the Saturday afternoon baseball games on TV and I imagined them calling my name and talking about me. But I didn't want to dream too much about it, think too much about it, because I knew I was a long shot. Everyone at the academy was going to be a long shot.

It wasn't long before my bags were packed and I was off to Sarasota, Florida, and even though I was excited, I was dreading it. I was leaving my wife and baby at home, and I had no idea what to expect once I got to the Academy. At least it wasn't going to be my first flight. I had taken a 20-hour train ride to Baton Rouge, Louisiana., to attend Southern University, and it didn't work out. I went down there with $500 to my name – I had $250 in one shoe and $250 in the other. Don't ask me why. That's what my parents told me I should do. This train stopped at every little town along the way, and I didn't think I was ever going to make it. I finally got there, got a room, enrolled and was ready to go when they told me I wasn't going to get any scholarship money. I couldn't go to school without a scholarship, so I went to the student union and saw a guy who had a Volkswagen. I asked him to drive me to the airport, and he did. I'd never flown before and really didn't know what to do. I went to a Delta terminal and bought a one-way ticket to Kansas City. When I got on the flight, there was a bunch of soldiers who were coming back home from Vietnam. I was impressed because I thought they were doing a great job, even though they didn't get much support at home. And I had lost a couple of friends over there, so I was honored to be with them on the flight, and it kind of took my mind off the fact that I had never been on a plane before and didn't know what to expect. I sat next to a soldier and we started talking. I told him I was going home because college didn't work out. We empathized with each other, about what we were going through, and he bought me a drink of liquor. I'd had a beer or two with my dad, but never any hard liquor. We landed at the downtown airport, my dad, who served in World War II, picked me up, and I was tipsy. He was pretty mad until I told him the story about how the soldier bought me a couple of drinks. He just said, "Okay, I understand, but let's not let your mom find out about this." And we drove home.

I was hoping my next plane trip would be a much more sobering experience - Sarasota, Fla., here I come! I didn't really have a lot of clothes, dressy clothes, to pack. I just took jeans, t-shirts, tennis shoes, stuff like that. That's all we really needed because we just went to class in the morning and played baseball in the afternoon. You just packed what you thought you needed, and as you went along you got a piece here and piece there. The flight was uneventful, and there was a bus to pick me up at the airport. I looked around and there were other players waiting to go to the Academy, so we kind of talked and wondered what we were getting into.

"Every day, since our opening on Aug. 10, 1970, it has been Christmas at the Kansas City Royals Baseball Academy…The gift might be a smile from one of the students suffering from homesickness, the next day it might be an improvement on the field. Or it might be searching questions asked during the classes at Manatee Junior College. The development of their skills has been great; matched only by their development as men. Never in my career have I seen a group of youngsters knit themselves into a family of poised and polished young men so quickly."

Syd Thrift
Academy director

When we got down there, the academy wasn't ready, so we stayed at the Sarasota Hotel, which was different. Then, when the dorms were ready and we moved into the Kansas City Royals Baseball Academy, everything changed – for the better. It was an exciting time. None of us knew what to expect, but we knew we were going to work hard – for the chance to play in the big leagues and for Mr. K, who was getting some bad letters from people who thought the academy would fail. I think it was so innovative – there was nothing like this back in 1970 – that people felt the need to slam Mr. K's idea. He got some really mean letters from other organizations, saying it was a dumb idea. They said scouts should be out finding players and that an academy wasn't going to be successful. I don't know about the other guys, but that fired me up. We pinned up those letters on our bulletin boards in the dorms, and in the locker rooms we used them as our source of inspiration.

It took a while to get regimented at the academy. Early on, there was a guy who wanted us to march onto the field, march around the academy grounds, that kind of stuff, and I thought to myself, *is this a baseball academy or the Army?* He didn't last long. Soon, we were getting up at 6 a.m. to eat breakfast. It was mandatory – which shows you how far ahead Mr. K was in his thinking. Now, everyone says breakfast is the most important meal of the day. He knew that back in 1970. If you didn't eat breakfast you got fined $10. You made $48 a month, so believe me, no one ever missed breakfast. We then went to Manatee Junior College and took classes until noon. Mr. K wanted us to go to school so we took general classes – math, history – I loved the psychology classes, the Dale Carnegie stuff. The only mandatory course that Mr. K made us take was public speaking because he thought that would be something we'd need once we got into Major League Baseball. Like I said, he was ahead of his time – way, way ahead of his time. Aretha Franklin was singing about respect, Three Dog Night and Creedence were big, and the student union was the place everyone was hanging out. It was a cool time to be alive.

"We realized that there was a long, tough road ahead of us, and there's a lot to be learned. But we have faith in the academy and faith in ourselves. When you finish high school and a scout hasn't come knocking on your door, a 7-year-old's dream becomes a 17-year-old's disappointment. But six months ago (when the academy opened), the impossible happened. It's the dream of a lifetime come true."

Sal Balderrama
Academy shortstop and longtime friend

When I got down to the academy, I heard some numbers that really surprised me. We had the tryout at Municipal Stadium, but there were 176 tryouts across the nation. They looked at 7,682 players and 35 wound up at the academy. Mr. K was sending the best of the best to his academy and we weren't going to let him down. I bet a lot of the Royals minor league guys were a little bit jealous of what we had, because we had 121 acres and five fields – and all of them were the same dimension as the new Royals Stadium that was being built (and would open in 1973). All the fields had turf, so we got used to that real quick. It was impressive. I didn't know what to expect when I got down there, but it was a lot more than I expected – and from talking to the other guys, it was more than they expected, too.

The instructors all had great baseball backgrounds. Joe Gordon, a Hall of Fame second baseman for the New York Yankees back in the

Joe DiMaggio era and the Royals first manager, was an instructor along with Bill Fischer, Tommy Henrich, Steve Korcheck, Jim Lemon, Johnny Neun, Chuck Stobbs – who gave up that mammoth home run Mickey Mantle hit out of Griffith Stadium – Frank Evans and Joe Tanner. Along with Buzzy Keller, Harry Ledford was our first trainer followed by Mickey Cobb, our trainer for many years in Kansas City (1977-1990). Willis Horton was also one of everyone's favorite guys.

We'd play a game a day, whether it was an inter-squad game or a game against a local college. We'd work on fundamentals quite a bit of the time and then we had mandatory study hall and lights out at 10. Fridays, we could stay up 'til 12 p.,m. And we could stay up 'to 2 a.m. on Saturdays, because we had Sundays off. And on Sundays, they opened up the academy for tourists to come visit.

We lived in dorms, and it was two players to a room. Myroomie was a kid from KCK who could really run. His name was Rufus Caruthers. We had our psychedelic posters on the walls and we thought we had the coolest dorm room in the academy. It was kind of funny,

About the only form of entertainment at the Royals Baseball Academy was this foosball table. When you were at the academy, they only wanted you thinking about baseball. But in our spare time we'd play some foosball or watch the one TV they had in the game room. We made $48 a month after taxes, so you didn't have a lot of money to spend on recreation.

but they wouldn't let you have your own television. They had one main TV in the lobby, and that was it. They told us that the reason they didn't want us to have TVs in our dorms was because they wanted us to do things in groups – we played pool or ping pong or watched TV together. This was all about bonding. We had maid service, which we really liked, and they even had umpires as part of the academy and they stayed in the dorms and served as hall monitors. Whenever Mrs. K came to visit – she was a big part of the academy because she picked out all the mattresses and furniture in the dorm rooms the maids would go through all the rooms and take down all the posters, especially the inappropriate ones, and put them in your closet. When she left, you could put them back on the wall.

Once we started playing, we were scoping each other out, trying to determine who the good players were going to be. I was married and was one of the oldest guys at 20. There were a lot of 17, 18 and 19 year olds and I had to make sure I worked hard so I stood out and people noticed me. I hit the first academy home run, stole a lot of bases, played well in the outfield – that's right, I went down there as an outfielder. That comment catches a lot of folks off guard because they think of me as a second baseman. I didn't care where they played me, as long as they played me and gave me the opportunity to prove myself. We were there from August through November and then got the chance to go home and see our families. We came back in January and started all over again. We played through the spring and we played as a team against some rookie league teams and we were something like 40-13 and finished second in the instructional league. I know Mr. K was proud of us, but we didn't have any time to celebrate. The next spring, you had to go out and make a minor league roster. I always thought we should have been an academy team, but I guess they wanted to see what we could do in a different environment.

"What the hell is that rattlesnake doing in my closet?"

Compared with today's technology, it's funny to look back at my time at the academy and think about one simple fact: We had a pay phone in the lobby and all the guys stood in line to use it. Today, I have two cell phones – and they are always ringing. But back then, that pay phone in the lobby was the lifeline to our families. Art and I were the only two married guys, so it meant even more to us. At night, we'd have dinner, go to the mandatory study hall then go back down to the cafeteria to wash dishes. By working in the cafeteria, we made about $14 a week extra, and that was our phone money. I figured it all out – I could call Kansas City and talk for three minutes and it cost me 12 quarters – $3. I called home every night and talked for three minutes. Gladys would ask a question, I'd ask a question and that was about it. Then it was time to hang up. Those three minutes got me through a lot of crazy stuff – like rattlesnakes in the outfield – and even in my dorm room closet.

When they built the Baseball Academy, it was in the middle of nowhere. It was five miles outside of Sarasota, on a two-lane road. There was a state park on one side and a couple of little lakes on the other side. It was nothing to see an alligator in the lake, or even coming out of the lake – that was okay, they were big and you could see them and keep away from them. But the rattlesnakes were a whole different problem. We'd go out on a hot afternoon and there on the pitcher's mound would be a rattlesnake all curled up. For $48 a month, I wasn't going to become the snake hunter. Usually, a grounds crew guy would go out with a rake or a bag or something and get the snake. We had white sand everywhere and you could see the snakes when they were crawling through the white sand, especially the white sand on the warning tracks in the outfield. I remember one day we had to stop a game because the left fielder wouldn't take his position because there was a rattlesnake out there.

I didn't know what the grounds crew did with the snakes until I came back to my dorm room one day and it smelled like hell. I mean, I'd never smelled anything like that smell . It made you gag and your eyes water and I'm thinking, "What on earth is in this room?" Earlier in the day, the grounds crew guys killed a snake, skinned it and ate the meat. You know what they say, it tastes like chicken…well, my roommate asked for the skin so he could make a belt out of it. I open the closet door and there, hanging in my closet, is that rattlesnake skin. The first thing I think is, "What the hell is that rattlesnake doing in my closet?"

It scared me to death. It was hanging from a hanger and I thought it was a live rattlesnake. I don't know why I didn't have a heart attack right then and there. When my roommate came back, I told him to get that thing out of there. He knew I was PO'd, and I don't think he ever did make a belt out of that skin. He took it down to the boiler room and the whole dorm suddenly smelled like our room. I don't know if he ever got his belt, but I told him he better not ever bring anything like that back into our dorm room.

We had a swimming pool and occasionally you would hear stories about alligators being in the pools, but I never saw one. None of us ever swam in the pool anyway because the water was always freezing. When they opened the academy, they took all these photos of girls in bikinis around the pool, which was the only time girls in bikinis were around the pools. They didn't pay much attention to a bunch of guys making $48 a month.

We were stuck in the middle of nowhere; we didn't have cars and we couldn't go anywhere – Mr. K knew what he was doing when he put that academy where he did. On Wednesday nights we'd get on a bus and go into Sarasota and eat pizza and catch a movie. Some of the guys did a pretty good job of sneaking their girlfriends back into the dorms. Their girlfriends might have cars and they would drive back with their car lights off and park a ways down the street and sneak into the dorm. But they usually got caught, and then we had some good stories to tell.

My biggest problem at the academy was being homesick. I don't know how many times I packed up my bags and said I was leaving. But I never did. Syd always talked me out of it. I wonder how many guys he had to talk out of leaving the academy. The second or third time I said I was leaving he told me something that kept me there – and I never thought about leaving again. He said Mr. K was going to give a $50,000 bonus to the first player from the academy to make it to the big leagues. It sounded good, but when I made it, the bonus never came.

I think Syd was just using that as incentive. I remember the first time I met Mr. K at the academy and he was wearing this Hickey Freeman, bright blue sports jacket and he said, "I'm a millionaire and I'm giving you guys an opportunity to live your dream and make a lot of money, too."

That was the first time I ever met a millionaire. And I just said, "Whoa! This cool." He went on to say how he was giving us the opportunity to not only play baseball, but get an education. But his goal was to get us in the big leagues. He wanted one of us in the big leagues when his new stadium opened in 1973.

I was part of the academy for 18 months, and it closed its doors in 1974. Was it a success? Well, for me, ABSOLUTLEY! Overall? I think so, yeah. I was lucky because I came into the academy knowing the basic fundamentals of the game. I had the good coaches in summer league ball and the good coaches in football and basketball at Lincoln High School. I knew how to field and throw the baseball, and I knew how to hit, and I knew I was going to have to work hard to improve in those areas, and I did. We had a certain amount of pitchers and fielders and we always played our intra-squad games with guys playing at their normal position. We worked hard, but in the back of all of our minds was the anticipation of making one of the Royals minor league teams after our first season at the academy.

I made the San Jose Rookie League team, and I did all right. I was with the Royals in spring training and Jack McKeon, who eventually became the Royals manager, wanted to take me up to AAA Omaha, but the team said no. They wanted me to get some seasoning in the lower minors. There were some people in the organization who really didn't support the academy idea. I don't think everyone wanted it to succeed, and there were some people who thought that I was older than 20. I remember Joe Tanner telling someone that he had to co-sign for a car I was buying. He never worried about how old I was. I had a higher skill level than most of the guys, but that's because of my work ethic and background.

When you were good and a minority, the perception was you were older than you really were. That was their mentality. It was a stereotypical thing. They kept wanting to see my birth certificate. Down in Mississippi, a birth certificate is filled in with a pencil. They didn't trust it. But I had Jack in my corner and that was a huge bonus.

San Jose was definitely interesting. You went from a confined dormitory to a town in California. It was exciting, and we had some good players on the team like (future Royals teammate) Al Cowens. All the guys on the team accepted me, except one – Roy Branch. He was a draft choice of the Royals and he kept giving me a hard time, taunting me, the typical stuff. So one night we're at a little pool hall and he's giving me a hard time, and we get into a fight. Everything changed after that night and I wasn't with the team much longer, as I got moved to AA Jacksonville, back in Florida.

Now in Sarasota, we were pretty much confined to the academy, but in Jacksonville, it was totally different. I was the only black player on the team and it caused some interesting situations. No, it created some uncomfortable situations for me and my teammates. We'd travel through the south and see the KKK signs. I wouldn't get off a bus at a lot of stops because of segregation, so my teammates would get me food and drinks and bring them to me on the bus. It took some getting used to, but I focused all my anger on improving my game and it worked because the next year I was in Omaha and later with the Royals. When I was in Omaha, I knew how close I was to making it to the big leagues.

I had a good, strong arm and I think that the Royals were fortunate for a long time because we had two shortstops playing up the middle – Freddie and me or U.L. and me. They had the arm strength – I had a strong arm, but their arms were stronger – but I could cover the ground at second base. We balanced each other out up the middle and gave the Royals a lot of years of pretty good defense.

Back then, and maybe even today, shortstop was the glamour position. But I wanted to make it in the big leagues and stay for a long time.

I finally made it up to AAA Omaha, and Harry Malmberg was the manager (McKeon had taken over as manager of the Royals). I went there as an outfielder, but I got to play some third and shortstop and they were impressed. I'll never forget one day when Harry came up to me and said, "I think you can be a good major league shortstop but you can be a great major league second baseman." I was playing a lot of shortstop for Harry when (Kansas City Royals all-star shortstop) Freddie Patek pulled a muscle in June and I got called up briefly.

"Welcome to the big leagues, rook."

My first big league game was in Baltimore. I came in, in the seventh inning and played shortstop. I heard much later on that the team didn't want me to come up, but Jack McKeon said, "Send me Frank, or don't send me anyone." I was excited that my first game was in Baltimore. The Orioles were one of my favorite teams and Frank Robinson was my favorite player. I wear No. 20 because of Frank. And they had a great shortstop in Mark Belanger, who had a string of seven straight Gold Gloves. He told me one time, "If you show me a shortstop who never sets his feet, I'll show you a bad shortstop."

They played at Memorial Stadium and it had these lights sitting right on top of the stadium. The first ball that was hit to me was a high

Turning the double play – that's such a great feeling when you get the perfect throw from your infield teammate and you are able to turn and throw the ball well before the runner comes bearing down on you. I loved turning those double plays, I really did.

chopper that I lost it in the lights and it hit me in the chest. What a way to start. I was thinking to myself, "I'm glad that didn't happen in Kansas City."

The next night against the Orioles I got my first big league hit and went 2-4. Jack started me again the next day and (Hall of Famer) Gaylord Perry was pitching. I had a double or triple and a sacrifice fly and my next at bat he knocks me down. He threw right at my head and flipped me. He flipped me good. I was on the ground and had all that dirt and lime (from the foul lines) in my mouth and eyes and I'm wondering what's going on. I'm lying on the ground and Hall of Fame umpire Nestor Chylak looks down at me and says, "Welcome to the big leagues, rook." I was steaming. Why had he thrown at my head? Coming out of the minors, I didn't know about things like that. Gaylord thought I was showing him up, so he threw at my head. Our guy on the mound, Dick Drago, then hit Chris Chambliss and broke his hand. He did it for me – he was protecting me and the rest of our hitters. I guess the Royals liked what I brought to the table. I felt pretty good about that – even though I didn't like to see a guy get hit and injured.

When I got up to the big leagues, I realized that Cookie (Rojas, the Royals all-star second baseman) was going to retire soon, so I went back down the minors and learned to play second base. It was hard – it was a lot different than shortstop, especially around the bag. When you complete a double play at short, you are going toward the bag, and when you're playing second, it's the exact opposite. I had a conversation with Tom Burgmeier (a former Royals pitcher) and we're talking about second base and shortstop and he said, "It's better to be a turd in the majors than a star in Triple A." What he meant was simple, I better work hard to find a way to stay in the big leagues. You can be the big fish in a little pond in the minors, but who cares? Guys were coming at you hard, it was a different game, and I had a lot to learn.

After the 1973 season, I played winter ball in Venezuela and Cookie was the manager. I learned to stay on the bag and be still. I caught the ball and got a peek at the base runner and made sure I didn't make the mistake of rushing the play. I know a lot of people say,

"Watch the speed of the runner at first," but I did everything off the speed of the ball coming off the bat. That determined whether I was going to try to make a double play or wasn't going to try to make a double play. I didn't want my third baseman or my shortstop deciding for me. Just get me the ball and let me make the decision. I learned to read the ball and that helped me make my decision on turning a double play.

Playing for Cookie was interesting. He was one of the better second baseman in baseball, but it wasn't unusual for players to go down and manage in winter ball. When I came up to the Royals, Cookie was a guy who didn't say anything to me. If veterans spoke to you, you could talk to them. But if they didn't say anything, you better not say anything to them. Everybody was real protective of their job.

That's my 100th career home run baseball and my last batting helmet. It's funny, when I was playing those things didn't mean that much to me. Now, they really mean a lot. It's fun to take guests downstairs to the family room and watch them look at the signed memorabilia, the Gold Gloves and some of my awards. The three baseballs on the right are signed by Lou Brock, Maury Wills and Joe DiMaggio. Lou, who starred with the St. Louis Cardinals, wrote: "To Frank, a long ball hitter." He must have remembered that home run I hit against his Cardinals in the 1985 World Series.

There was no free agency, everybody was on a one-year contract, so nobody's eager to have someone take their job. He made a play one day and I remember going up to him on the bench and asking about the play. It was probably something to do with a double play, more than anything else. And I asked him about it and he didn't give me an answer. He just stared ahead and I asked him again, thinking he didn't hear me. When he didn't answer the second time, I got the message. So I decided to ask him the same question every day until I got an answer. Finally, he said, "Look I know you're playing winter ball and I'm going to be managing in Venezuela. Come play for me and we can work on what you want to work on." That was his challenge to me and I said okay, I'll take it. I went down to Venezuela and went out every day and worked at second base. He never agreed with how I fielded the ball, because I was always taught to field forward through the ball while most people are cradling the ball, and I remember one day we were playing catch and he said that you have to cradle the ball like an egg and I said "This is not an egg." I got one of those eye rolls like he was thinking, "Yeah, smart ass rookie." But he still worked with me, especially on the double plays. He taught me some shortcuts. We worked on being able to concentrate on the throw until I got the ball, and then made the throw to first base rather than trying to peek too soon and drop the ball. We never met early and had any special stuff, just the normal routine before a game. And I was fine with that. He was a good teacher. He wouldn't have been managing in winter ball if he didn't want to teach and make the game better, the players better, even the heir apparent to replace him.

When I got called up to replace Freddie, I felt some pressure, even though Dick Drago made sure no one threw at my head while he was on the mound. The first time I walked into the locker room, Big John (Mayberry, the team's all-star first baseman) says, "Well, if it isn't Academy Frank." I had to earn his respect and I had to earn the respect of the rest of my teammates. I felt extra pressure to do well since I was the first one of Mr. K's academy players to make the major leagues, but there is pressure to make the team and stay with the team. I knew this was just until Freddie was healthy and ready to come back, but I got a taste of the big leagues and I liked it. I played with a chip on my shoulder because I had to prove that even though I didn't get drafted for $30,000 dollars, I was a good ball player. And I think that's where the edge came from. My dad always had an edge, and I was discovering that I had that edge, too.

Ron (Washington, who played in the big leagues but never with the Royals) and U.L. (Washington, who played shortstop with the Royals), had that edge. That "Academy Frank" name followed me until I was able to prove myself. And I did prove myself, and even though I came from the academy, it didn't really seem to matter as I became more successful at the big league level. I remember a conversation I had with Royals head scout Art Stewart, who told me that Mr. K told him that he faced a cost issue with the academy, and that the worst thing he ever did was close it down in 1974. Who knows what kind of talent it might have produced. You look at the teams today who have similar academies in the Dominican Republic or urban youth academies – Mr. K was the first to do it, and I will always be appreciative.

5 "The House that White Built? Not exactly."

WHEN I WAS A KID, MY BEST FRIEND LEON SLAUGHTER AND I WOULD walk past Municipal Stadium on our way to school and back home. You dreamed of playing in the stadium, but you knew the odds were against you. Now, I'm in the minors and Mr. K gets me a job working at his new stadium. And there's the chance that I might actually play in this stadium. That's hard to imagine. Looking back on it, it's even harder to imagine, to believe something like that could happen to a kid from Kansas City.

I mean it was pretty exciting, because you're working on a part of a new stadium and you're in the minor leagues and you're hoping that you're going to be one of those guys who make that place special for the baseball fans of Kansas City.

I remember a lot of nights and hot afternoons when I was working on the third deck and we were sealing floors and I would come out, look down at the field and imagine myself playing down there. I didn't know whether I saw myself as a shortstop or second baseman back in those days, but I saw myself. I thought maybe if I wished hard enough, it would happen. Then I thought, if I worked hard enough it would happen, and the hard work had a lot more to do with it than the wishing.

I was going to spring training with the Royals, and who knows what might happen. I knew I was going to go to the big leagues, but it didn't happen as I was the last player cut, and that was hard to overcome. But I got called up in June to replace Freddie Patek when he got injured and I felt like I showed them enough that this could be my year. I got called up on the road, so it was different from getting called up and looking at this stadium. This stadium I helped build, knowing that my family and friends were here to support me. I'm sealing the floor, scraping mortar, dreaming. Some of my friends say they should call it "The House that White Built."

The House that White Built? Not exactly. I had to earn that. When I look at the columns on the main level, I think back to the day when I had a chisel and a machine and I scraped off all the concrete overflow. It was hard work, but I was used to hard work – and I was making good money. This is how much baseball has changed over the years – I was on a construction crew at Royals Stadium and I was making more money than I ever dreamed of making with the Royals. I made $750 a month at AAA Omaha. When I got called up to the Royals, the minimum salary was $14,000. That seemed like so much money. My only real splurge was a 1973 Dodge Charger. It was white. It was sweet. Gladys, Frank and I lived in a kitchenette on the corner of 29th and Paseo. We rented it, and eventually my dad bought the house next to him and we moved into it. We lived on the third floor and had a lot more space. When it looked like I had made the team, we eventually moved to Blue Springs. I still, to this day, don't know what would have happened if Mr. K wouldn't have allowed me to go the academy as a married guy, if Gladys wouldn't have said yes when I asked her about going, and if she hadn't gotten that job at the stadium in the ticket office.

Gladys and I met the last day of school in 1968. We had just graduated from high school and I was actually trying to date one of her friends, who gave me the cold shoulder. She lived at 29th and Paseo, and I asked if I could walk her home. There was a basketball court on 29th Street and we were always down there playing and I'd see Gladys down there near her home. She was a majorette for the football team, and she'd be down there twirling her baton. I started talking to her and we just hooked up. We were married a year later in October of 1969. My mom and dad really liked Gladys. She was quiet and fun to be around. We lived with my parents and it worked out well. Frank was born in August of 1969 and that's a life-changing experience. Frank was always surrounded by a lot of love – whether it be from me and Gladys or my parents or aunts and his uncle. It was a good situation. But it was a tough time too, because I headed out to the academy and the phones weren't as sophisticated as they are now, and I didn't get to watch him grow up and take part in his summer activities like I would have liked to. But I was trying to make a living playing baseball and he understood that. Even at a young age I think he understood. I always wanted to take care of my family first, and by playing baseball, I was able to do that.

When I got to the majors, the base salary was $14,000. The base salary today is something like $430,000 to $450,000. That's why we had to form unions and have players make sacrifices so we had the freedom to move from one team to another and to make a better life for ourselves and our families. Every player should know about Curt Flood and the sacrifices he made for future generations of players. They should know about how we got free agency and started making good money. There are a lot of players – black, white, Latino – who don't even know the real story of Jackie Robinson. And that just amazes me.

I guess I'm not a sentimental guy, but when I played in Royals Stadium, I never really thought about working there, from 8 a.m. to 5 p.m. on the construction crews. It was a job, a very good job, and I gave

There are three generation of Whites in that photo – Frank Sr., Frank Jr., and Frank III. That photo was taken a few years ago when they named the Lee's Summit Sports Complex after me. That was a great honor, and it was an even greater honor to share it with my father and my oldest son.

Mr. K everything I had whether I was pouring concrete, sealing floors or turning a double play. All I wanted was a chance, the opportunity to show everyone I could play. I'd take it from there – and I was getting that opportunity thanks to Mr. K and his academy. It seemed like such a long time ago when Leon and I would stand on the top of the football bleachers at Lincoln High School and watch games at Municipal Stadium. George Toma (the Royals Hall of Fame groundskeeper) used to open a gate in left field at some games and let us in so we could see the whole stadium. I'll never forget how beautiful it was – it was the most beautiful thing a kid who loved baseball could ever see. And I wanted this new stadium to be even better. I could close my eyes and imagine the cheers. If I tried hard enough, I could hear the fans cheering, and I could see my mom, dad, and brother and sisters in the stands. The only thing better than thinking about it, was making it happen.

6 "We were an expansion team that never finished in last place."

PEOPLE LIKE TO TALK ABOUT 1976 AS THE BEGINNING OF SOMEthing special, and I can't argue with that. But the years 1973 through 1975 were special, too. We were an expansion team, and expansion teams are supposed to get beat up a little bit. And we did – but we didn't get beat up as much as some teams. That intrigued me. When you look back at those teams you could see a team being built that had the perfect blend of athletic ability, pitching, defense and hitting. You know what impressed me about the Royals in the early days? We were an expansion team that never finished in last place. We had George and Freddie and Big John and Amos and Cookie and pitchers like Busby and Splittorff. I would soon take over for Cookie at second and join Al Cowens, a tough kid from Compton, California, who had a cannon for an arm. With Big John at first, me at second and Cowens in right field, we had the best right side defense in the league. And our pitchers appreciated that. Eventually, Willie came along and you could just see the athletic ability coming together. And I think the fact that we held our own as we grew and developed as a team, gave us that much more confidence that we could get it done. And then in '76 we really put it together. We had a big lead at the all-star break but we still hadn't crossed that bridge to get to the playoffs. We eventually backed into the playoffs when Oakland lost, but you could see the confidence and the mental toughness growing and developing. We learned how to win in 1973 through 1975, and in 1976 we went out and won. And in 1977 we had the best regular season in the history of the team. That wasn't by accident. We had a good mix of young guys and veterans and we had a team that was perfect for Royals Stadium. We hit a lot of balls in the gaps and we had good pitching, we had it all. And I think because of our range and ability, the whole dynamics of the game changed when Cowens and I played together on the right side of the field. I never ran into one of our right fielders my whole career with the Royals – and that's remarkable. We knew how to play, we knew how to make the job easy for the other guy, and we were pros. Cowens and I both won Gold Gloves in 1977, and the best was yet to come.

And talkin' about the best yet to come... take a look at this action.

6

Some of guys on the team, who really put it all together in 1976, had a bad season in 1973. Hal had problems and started working with our hitting coach, Charley Lau, who became so famous for helping George become one of the best clutch hitters of all time and a three-time batting champion. Guys struggled, but they never gave up. George and Hal worked to refine their swings and in 1976 George edged Hal on the last day of the season for the American League batting championship that ended in controversy. There was a feeling among some players that the Twins left-fielder misplayed Brett's hit on purpose to keep Hal from winning the title. Back then, I wasn't an everyday guy, so I just took it all in. When they needed me, I was ready. But I had the best seat in the house to watch the development and growth of a team that would dominate over the next 10 years. When it all unfolds like you hoped it would, you just sit back and enjoy every minute of it. The years leading up to that first division championship were as special to me as going to the playoffs, because I enjoyed the process. I enjoyed watching veterans Cookie, Freddie and Amos. We went to Oakland and needed a win to clinch a tie in the division in 1976, and we got it done. We finally clinched at home when they lost, but that was bittersweet for me, but I was happy. I didn't know what the future had in store for the team. I didn't know we'd win more games in the regular season the next year than any other team or make the playoffs three years in a row or go to the World Series in 1980.

Just speaking for me, I was looking forward to winning that game that got us in the playoffs. You work so hard during the regular season, and I think we all deserved that win so we could celebrate with each other. It happened – the very next year – and getting it done with your teammates makes it even sweeter.

7

"Every day, to and from school, we'd walk past Municipal Stadium, where the Kansas City A's played. And we'd lay our hands on the wall of the stadium and dream about playing there someday."

PEOPLE ARE ALWAYS ASKING ME WHAT IT WAS LIKE TO PLAY MY first game at Royals Stadium, and I have to be honest with you – I don't even remember it. Before I did a little research, I always thought we'd played a doubleheader against Oakland, but I was wrong. We played a series against the A's – it was the year they won the World Series – and it took three games before we won a home game. My first home game was June 18, 1973, and we lost 9-5. I hit in the leadoff position, played shortstop and was 0-4. I was part of two double plays.

I do remember that it was fun coming home and seeing my family and friends after we'd been on the road. The game was a big deal to me. I did get my first base hit at home the next night in an 11-6 loss to the A's. Once again, Jack McKeon had me hitting leadoff, and I was 2-for-5 with a run scored. I don't remember anything special about that game. I don't have the ball from my first hit at home – I have the ball from my first hit in the big leagues. I was a baseball player, that was my job, and I wanted to be good at it. I wasn't thinking about being in a headline in The Star – Hometown Kid Returns to Kansas City – those things happen today when they bring up a big-time draft pick like (Eric) Hosmer or (Mike) Moustakas, but that didn't happen back then. Really, you just shared all that with your family and friends.

"If Frank and I didn't have a ball, we'd still find a way to play baseball or stick ball," said Leon Slaughter, Frank's best friend since their childhood days in the neighborhood. "We had a baseball that we played with so much, we wore it down to that little, hard rubber ball in the core of the baseball. I remember using a ball from the game jacks – those small rubber balls – and we'd hit it with a stick. Then, Frank would get one of the heads off his sisters' dolls and we'd use that, too. They weren't very happy about it, but we had to play ball – it was in our blood.

"Every day, to and from school, we'd walk past Municipal Stadium, where the Kansas City A's played. And we'd lay our hands on the wall of the stadium and dream about playing there someday. We all knew it would happen for Frank –he was that much better than everyone else. He was special, an all-around guy, and he was my best friend. We lived a block from each other and we went to Lincoln Jr. and Sr. high schools together. We walked to school and talked about sports. If we weren't in school and talking about sports, we were playing something. Spring Valley Park was our second home.

"We played at Paseo Park off Truman Road. We'd walk there and get a ten cent chili dog at a little place called the Candy Kitchen at 18th and Vine. We were so close – you could have called me Leon White and Frank, Frank Slaughter. We went to senior prom together – I took a date and Frank took Gladys, and my mother gave me the keys to her car. She knew I didn't drive that well, but we made it. Like I said, we did everything together. I talked with Frank when the Royals offered him the chance to go to the academy. I told him he had to go, he had to try to make that dream come true.

"And when he made it, I was elated. The entire neighborhood was elated, because we all loved Frank. When someone from the neighborhood made it big, we all felt like we made it. When he played for the Royals, we were all there. I'd sit behind the plate, or stand up on the rail with his father and his friends. We wanted Frank to know we were there for him and that we would support him, no matter what happened. We knew he'd make it and we knew he'd be good, because he had such a work ethic. I don't remember the specific games with Frank, I just remember how much fun it was, watching my best friend, play baseball for the hometown team."

The same could be said for Frank's brother and four sisters.

"I have to admit that I am the baby of the family and I idolized my brother Frank," said Faye Bogges, Frank's youngest sister. "But he

By the look on my face, I think I just hit one out of the park. That's such a great feeling – especially when you're hitting cleanup in the 1985 World Series and hit a homer in our first win. I wasn't known for the long ball, but I managed to muscle up a time or two.

did one thing that made me cry. If he couldn't find a baseball to play with, he would take one of the hard, plastic heads off my baby dolls – the kind that had the plastic heads and soft cloth bodies – and use that for a ball. I'd go crying to mama and there Frank would be in the back alley, using my doll's head for a ball. I guess you could say our dolls helped Frank reach his dream of playing professional baseball.

"When he made the Royals, I was always introduced as Frank White's sister, and I finally had to say, 'I have a name. I am Frank White's sister, but I have a name – Faye.' Everyone loved being around Frank, and I would always say that he is a reflection of our parents. They were so proud of him, we're all proud of him. He was a great player and he is a great man."

Like her younger sister Faye, Joyce White recalls some incidents when she and her sisters would ask Frank about the missing heads of their dolls.

"Frank beheaded our dolls," laughs Joyce. "Faye and I would get so upset, but that was the only time we'd get upset with Frank. He was 10 years older than me, and I always saw him as my big brother, and nothing else. We were not a boastful family, we were a loving family, but we were all so proud of Frank. When I was a young woman in the dating scene, I looked for someone just like my older brother. He watched over us and took care of us. Even if he did use our doll heads to play ball in the alley, we loved him.

"He was a good big brother and he is such a wonderful man today. We were in Memphis at a family reunion and we were at a restaurant and you know that movie, 'Made in America,' where Eddie Murphy is a king in his country and he comes to the United States? Well, there is a scene where he is standing in line, he is recognized by someone, and they just go crazy when they see him. We're at this restaurant and a man from Kansas City recognizes Frank and he just goes crazy, he is so excited to meet Frank. It reminded me of that scene from the movie. Whenever Frank is recognized or someone wants to meet him and shake his hand or get a photo or autograph, he is so polite and gracious. I just take so much pride in being his sister, I really do."

Diane White and her sisters knew one thing about their older brother – if they received a doll for Christmas, they better enjoy the moment, because the moment he needed a baseball those doll heads were his.

"We'd get a doll for Christmas," Diane said, "and two days after Christmas the heads were gone. We knew where they were – back in the alley where Frank was playing baseball with them. He would take anything he could find and make a baseball out of it. I think if anyone else would have done that we would have been mad – but it was impossible to get mad at Frank. He was a special big brother – all the girls felt that way. We've grown up with him, watching him develop from one of the best athletes and most popular kids in the neighborhood to a baseball player with the Kansas City Royals. We're proud of everything he does, but I'm most proud of the way he treats his fans and the people

Here I am with two of my favorite people. The guy in the middle, who always looks so dapper, is Negro Leagues Baseball Museum executive director Bob Kendrick and you probably recognize the guy on the right – that's the Wizard of Oz, St. Louis' Hall of Fame shortstop Ozzie Smith. We were at the Negro Leagues Baseball Museum taking part in a special ceremony where Negro Leagues members were presented with their own unique Gold Gloves.

in the neighborhood. He has time for everyone, and he's always been like that."

Mona Young was the sister closest in age to her older brother. "He was so protective – and he still is," Mona said. "Because I was close to Frank's age, we went to school together and I would follow him down the halls or I'd walk behind him if he was walking home with a girl. I just idolized him. I played ball, and I think Frank enjoyed that I played softball and was always out playing some kind of ball, too. We didn't have a whole lot when we were growing up, but we never knew it. We had love, and that was more important than anything else.

"I remember going to Royals games, watching Frank, and I was so proud of him. Me and my little girl friends would go – and it would bother me sometimes when an usher or someone would ask to see our ticket stubs to make sure we belonged in our seats. I told them that I was Frank's sister and that we got the seats from him, and they would look at us like they didn't believe me. But that didn't happen that often, and nothing could take away the joy we got from watching Frank play."

Vernon White is three years older than Frank, and he offers a unique view of watching his younger brother's journey from Spring Valley Park to Royals Stadium. "It was wonderful watching Frank grow up, just wonderful," Vernon said. "He always was playing some sort of sport – football and basketball in high school and baseball in the summer. And he was such a good young man and such a fine athlete.

"When that limousine came to our house and Mr. K wanted to talk to Frank about the academy it was just pandemonium in our house and in the neighborhood. We'd never seen a limousine up close and there was Frank, sitting in that limousine talking to an important man like Mr. K. We were so proud, we knew Frank was going to be special, and he was – and still is today."

Vernon paused for a moment, and added, "You know, all the girls in the family think Frank always took their dolls heads to play baseball. But I did a few times, too. I liked playing ball with Frank back in the alley, too, and when we ran out of balls, we got those doll heads. They were better than nothing."

Vernon's proudest moment came in 1985 when he watched his younger brother hit cleanup in the World Series against the Cardinals. "Oh, man, that was special," Vernon said. "I never went in the locker room or did any of that stuff, but watching Frank win a World Series was the best feeling. And that is the way our neighborhood felt and all of Kansas City felt after the Royals won it. I think I'll remember that more than what Frank did in the World Series. He made his community proud. And that's what makes me proud to have Frank as a brother – he's always finding a way to make us proud."

8

"I think going to Yankee Stadium in 1976 was a lot more intimidating than it is now because the fans were a lot rowdier and were very disrespectful."

WE FINALLY MADE THE PLAYOFFS IN 1976 AND HAD TO FACE THE NEW York Yankees, which began a rivalry that might have been one of the best in baseball over the next decade. We didn't like them and they didn't like us. And the playoff games were amazing – and heartbreaking. In 1976 I was a utility guy, so Cookie played most of the games and I got to watch the action. We lost the first playoff game at home and the Yankees beat Larry Gura 4-1. Larry was kind of our Yankee killer and that was surprising. We were all fired up, thinking we could take two games at home and just need to win at Yankee Stadium. We followed that loss with a 7-3 win and Splittorff looked great. So it's off to New York. I think going to Yankee Stadium in 1976 was a lot more intimidating than it is now because the fans were a lot rowdier and very disrespectful. They win 5-3, so we face a must-win situation the next night and Doug Bird comes on in relief of Gura and we beat Catfish Hunter 7-4. That set the stage for one of the most heartbreaking games I ever played in my life. The score was tied 6-6 in the bottom of the ninth inning. George and Big John had hit homers and we kept fighting back and fighting back and tied the score, but Chris Chambliss hit a game-winning homer off Mark Littell, and I think every fan in that stadium ran out on the field. It was crazy, it was scary. I don't know how Chambliss made it around the bases and I don't know how our guys made it off the field. I was sitting on the bench with chill bumps, because the way we kept coming back, I knew we were going to find a way to win. But it didn't happen. I had the same feeling that night in Oakland, when we needed to get a win to clinch the division and we lost three in a row. Gura finally got us a win and eventually we backed into the playoffs, but to go from such a high to such a low is tough. When Chambliss hit that home run, people stormed the field. We had people climbing over the dugout, falling into the dugout, pandemonium. They were digging up big pieces of grass, taking handfuls of dirt, grabbing the bases...I remember Reggie Jackson taking his hat and stuffing it inside his shirt. I don't know how Chambliss made it all the way around the bases. His teammates were there at home plate to greet him and protect him. The Yankees and Major League Baseball found out that day that if 58,000 people want to storm the field and do whatever they want, they're going to do it. After that game, security got a lot tougher, but they were still the craziest fans in baseball.

That game really inspired us to come out and have a great 1977 season, and we did. We had the best season in the history of the team. We were still heartbroken, but we showed a lot of resolve. I think it was just a great character team, and we were still thinking about Chambliss' homer. It would have been so much fun to play the Dodgers in the World Series. We were kind of patterned after the Dodgers – our uniforms, our stadium – a lot of stuff. So that would have been an interesting matchup. But for a young team to make it that far was special. The Yankees had been in so many playoff games and World Series, they knew how to win. We were still learning. And we were learning at a rapid pace.

We ran away with the division championship and played the Yankees again, and this time, we thought it would be a different outcome. And it couldn't have started out any better as we won the first game 7-2 and Splitt pitched a complete game for the win. But Ron Guidry pitched a complete game in Game 2 and the Yankees won 6-2 to send the series back to Kansas City for the final three games.

There was no doubt we were going to win two of those games. The entire second half of the season we couldn't do anything wrong, and that's how the ALCS started with that first win in New York.

We came home and Dennis Leonard pitched another complete game and we won 6-2. We were so confident going into Game 5, we just knew we were going to win and go to our first World Series. But it didn't happen – and that game was one I'll never forget for a lot of reasons. We lost 6-4, and it was just a nightmare. There were a lot of things surrounding that game, and they had to do with Big John. We played in the afternoon and John came in late. And he really wasn't what you would consider ready to play. He said it was because of a bad tooth, but he was a little shaky at the plate and at first base. He struck out a couple of times, missed a pop up and a throw at first base and Whitey (Herzog, the Royals manager) was furious. He never let go of that, and he pulled John from the game and benched him for Game 5. That was the game we needed our guys, so everybody went into Whitey's office and we told him that Big John was ready to play in Game 5 and that we needed our best team out on the field to beat the Yankees. We told Whitey to deal with his feelings for John later, but to put the best team out there to win Game 5. He refused and started Pete LaCock at first base. Some guys on the team agreed with Whitey and some didn't. I wanted the best guys on the field, and even though John was not one of the best guys in Game 4, we knew he could come back strong. When I think back to that 1977 season, I think of Big John's problems in Game 4 – which led to the team getting rid of him in the offseason – and our 3-2 lead in the top of the ninth inning in Game 5. We had the lead and Whitey did everything he could to win that game. He used Leonard and Gura – two starters – in the ninth inning in relief, but the Yankees scored three runs and we lost 5-3. I remember wondering why Whitey brought in Leonard. He was always a slow starter – it took him a while to get warmed up, but once he was warmed up, he was the best in the game. We were looking for Mickey Rivers to bunt and he got ahead in the count and hit a ball up the middle for the big base hit of the inning. He took Splitt out of the game early, I think in the sixth or seventh and he was pitching well. Those are the things you start thinking about after you lose. If we would have won, no one would have questioned anything, even Big John sitting on the bench.

The loss in New York in 1976 was tough, especially watching their fans go crazy and celebrating. But this one was even tougher. It was a kick to the gut. After the game was over, Amos and Mac (Hal McRae) and I went over to the Holiday Inn and told our wives that we wouldn't be home right away and we went over and closed the bar. We knew we were going to win that game, and we didn't. It was the worst defeat ever for me, and I'm talking about every game I'd played since Little League. I wondered how we were going to get over that loss.

We talked, and drank and talked some more. The Chambliss home run, the lead in the ninth at home and they score three runs to win. We finally figured it out. The Yankees were finishers, and they were winners. We had to find a way to finish out a series. Prior to 1976, the Yankees weren't a powerhouse (in the 1970s). But they went to the free agent market and got guys who knew how to win. They had guys like Sparky Lyle and Goose Gossage, and guys who would find a way to win when you couldn't.

Once again, we make a promise to ourselves that we're going to win the division, and if we meet the Yankees again in the ALCS, we're not going to lose to them in Game 5.

We lost it in Game 4.

The entire playoffs are just a blur – I guess, because I was trying to forget what happened to us for the third ALCS in a row. I think we wanted to play the Red Sox, but the Yankees beat the Red Sox in a one-game playoff when Bucky Dent hit the game-winning homer off Mike Torrez. When the Yankees won that game, it was like, "Here we go again." We felt like we had a much better chance against a team like Boston because they weren't a turf team and it was just a new playoff opponent. We really didn't want to play the Yankees again, and it showed. Jim Beattie pitched the first game for the Yankees, and we didn't know anything about him. They won 7-1 and that pretty much set the tone for the entire series. It's scary going into a series and facing a pitcher you don't know anything about. Not using that as an excuse, that's just what happened. We come back and win the second game 10-4 with Gura on the mound, and you begin to think, well, who knows what's going to happen? But we go to their place and lose 6-5 and 2-1. Gossage pitches the last three innings in the Game 3 win, and Guidry outduels Leonard in Game 4. We just couldn't do anything against Guidry in that game. When you played the Yankees, it was like you better get your runs in seven innings, because Gossage is going to come in and pitch the last couple of innings and game over! That was how the game used to be. You put your best guy in and used him when you needed him. Then it changed, and I think it changed because of money. You were paying a set up guy, so you had to use him. If you had a starter pitching well, you had to take him out to bring in the closer. I think set up guys and closers are important – look what Gossage meant to the Yankees – but if you have a guy with the hot hand, go with him. Today, the guys get saves by coming into the game in the ninth inning with no one on base. That wasn't the case with Gossage, (Rollie) Fingers, Quisenberry guys like that. They earned their saves because they rarely started an inning – they came in when everything was on the line.

In pro sports, it's all about winning a championship. To climb a mountain, you have to keep putting one foot in front of the other until you get to the top and flip over onto the other side. We didn't have a problem getting to the top, but we had a hard time throwing that leg across the top getting to the other side. I kept asking myself why that happened. We worked hard. I'm sure we worked as hard as the Yankees

That's one of my 1970s promo photos from the Royals. I'd say it's from 1977 or 1978. Those were some good days, and I had plenty of reasons to smile back then.

than we were. I think it was like our rivalry with the A's. For years, they were a little bit better than we were, then in 1976 we got past them and went into the playoffs. We did it the next two years – but we couldn't find a way to win the big game. I think the tough losses make you stronger, but that's tough to deal with. We were a team, in every sense of the word. We would stand up for each other and do anything to win. But year after year after year we lost to a team that was more aggressive in the free-agent market, and did what it took to be a champion. I wanted to be a champion – so did Mac and George and Duke and Amos – all the guys who had been through all the battles. When I think back, the one area I think the Yankees had the big edge was the bullpen – Gossage and Lyle. I liked our guys in the pen, but we didn't have Gossage and Lyle. A lot changed when we got Quiz (all-star closer Dan Quisenberry). Whitey was doing everything he could to beat the Yankees, but when he brought in Leo in the ninth inning against the Yankees we were all just kind of looking at each other wondering what was going on. Leo was probably the best starter in the league, but he wasn't a reliever. You just felt like nothing good was going to come from that move. Then we lose the ALCS in four games in 1978 and all the changes come. Whitey forces Mr. K to trade big John to Toronto and a lot of the guys were upset about that trade. John was hitting home runs in Toronto and Whitey moved Clint Hurdle from right field to first base and Clint couldn't handle the pressure of replacing a guy like John Mayberry, and that wasn't fair to a young guy like Hurdle. The fans loved Big John, Mr. K loved Big John and we loved playing with him. He was the glue in the infield. He helped me win some Gold Gloves and I know he helped the other guys, too. He made it easy for us, and he was such a presence in the locker room. A lot of people look at Game 4 and say Big John cost us the playoffs, but you can look at Game 5 and say that it cost us the playoffs by not having Big John in the game. That's a debate that has no answer. We all wish things like that would have never happened, but that's life. You deal with it and you move on.

What I kept wondering was if we were ever going to climb that mountain, get to the top, and stay there. In 1976 I thought we were the better team, but we didn't prove it in the playoffs. In 1977 we were the best team in baseball, but the Yankees still beat us. In 1978 we were thinking about the Red Sox and the Yankees come back and beat them in the playoff game and we lose to the Yankees in four games. If you just sit and think about that stuff, it can drive you crazy. What we needed to do was keep working, get some better players, and play as a team. When you think about all the tough playoff losses from 1976, 1977 and 1978 – then you look at years like 1980 when we make it to the World Series and lose to the Phillies, in 1981 where we lost the mini-playoffs to the A's because of the strike, then 1983 with the drug scandal, you get to wondering if it's ever going to happen. We had a lot of shots at doing something special, but we never reached the ultimate goal.

When you look back over our history, we won a lot, but we also lost a lot of tough games in crucial situations. We were a successful franchise. But Mr. K didn't spend money like a lot of the other owners. It's his team, and he can do what he wants with his money. Look at the situation today. It would be much, much more difficult to play on a team that doesn't have a chance of making the playoffs than playing on a team that gets so close, but never grabs the golden ring. If we would have been more aggressive in the free agent market, I think things would have been a lot different. No one even cared about the Yankees until (owner) George Steinbrenner started bringing in all those big-name guys, the top free agents. How can you compete with that? We were a team that did a great job developing guys through the farm system. We made decent money, but not the type of money the top guys with the Yankees were making. If we would have been more aggressive with the free-agent market, I think a lot would have changed for us. Who knows how many championships we might have won.

You look back at the mid 1970s and I think some of the big-name free agents would have come here to play. We were playing in front of 39,000 to 40,000 every game and people would come from all over the Midwest to watch us. We weren't just a team that was supported by Kansas Citians, we had people come in from a 150-mile radius to watch us. We had turf, so the games wouldn't get rained out that often, we had a beautiful new stadium, and we had some great players. If you drove down from Omaha, you knew you were going to see Leonard or Splittorff or Amos or George or me – and it was that way for years. And we were a fun team to watch. We played great defense, had speed, talent - we had it all. We just couldn't close the deal. When you fail three times in a row and then don't make the playoffs in 1979, you begin to doubt yourself and your team.

9 "Family, friends, fans, wherever you went, people were saying, 'You guys can't let this happen again, we gotta win this.'"

IT'S 1980, AND WE'RE BACK IN THE PLAYOFFS. AFTER 1976, 1977 and 1978, all we can ask for is another shot. You can look back and think about this play, or this decision, or this game and it doesn't matter because it's in the past and it's time to move on. I think the toughest loss was 1977 because we were a very good team that didn't get it done in the playoff. Then, we're all watching that one-game playoffs between the Yankees and Red Sox – and all through the last part of the season we're thinking we're going to be playing Boston – and Bucky Dent hits the homer off Torrez and it's like, here we go again. And then we lose to Jim Beattie, a guy we knew nothing about , and the frustration just begins to boil over. In the back of my mind, I'm thinking that I just want to play someone else. I'm tired of playing the Yankees in the playoffs. No, let me put that another way – I'm tired of losing to the Yankees in the playoffs. I'm tired of being the bridesmaid. I'm tired of never being able to get over the hump in the games that matter the most.

I don't know if Royals fans today really know what it's like to have a real rivalry with a team like we had with the Yankees. I was talking with Reggie about that when he came to town during the All-Star Game. When we finally started winning, he signed with the Yankees. He wasn't on the 1976 Yankees, but he was there in 1977 and 1978 and he had the huge World Series performances – hit those three home runs in the game against the Dodgers in 1977. We talked about the rivalries and how intense it was when our teams played. I was amazed at how much he knew about our team. He is a student of the game. He started naming off guys on the team, what they did against the Yankees – he remembered everything. We didn't like the

Yankees, but we respected them as a team. You have to respect a team that does what they did to us for those three years. They always found a way to beat us, and Reggie talked a lot about that – about that winning approach and how they did whatever it took to win. Now, looking back on the 1980 American League Championship Series, we knew we had to do something special, we had to find a way to win that darn thing.

I think one reason I enjoyed visiting with Reggie so much was because baseball was different back then. In those days, you really couldn't fraternize with the other team very much. The umpires used to be in the stands during batting practice and if you'd talk to the other team too long they'd whistle at you and tell you to move along. And then if you'd stay too long, you'd get a letter in the mail informing you that you'd been fined $50 for fraternizing. You'd send $50 to the league and they'd give it to a charity – but that's how it was. We didn't really know those guys on the Yankees like players know each other today, and I think that's one reason the rivalry was so strong. Guys played with the same team for most of their career, there wasn't a lot of movement of players from one team to another, and we just had one collective goal – find a way to beat the Yankees. There was pressure before every ALCS, but this year it was different. We were 0-3 against the Yankees in the playoffs, we missed the postseason in 1979, and there was a real sense of desperation, of urgency. Family, friends, fans, wherever you went, people were saying, "You guys can't let this happen again, we gotta win this."

I told myself I'm going into this series and I'm not looking back. I'm not going to think about the Chambliss homer, the ninth-inning collapse the next year or all the stuff that happened in the third game of the 1978 championship series. Yeah, right – I was thinking about that stuff and it made me even more determined to make sure we did something positive this time around.

Before Game 1 in 1980, the pressure was just building and building. I couldn't sleep the night before. I got up and went to the ballpark at 6:30-7:00 in the morning, got on the training table and slept like a baby for a couple of hours. I figured that's where I needed to be. And I think that in the case of other players, you didn't have as much, you know, joking around, guys were more intense, guys were more in their locker, focusing on the job at hand, and I think everybody was feeling the same thing but just not saying it. And everybody was just waiting for the game to start. It was a different atmosphere than I was used to.

Larry was going for us and we were excited that he was going to be on the mound. He was our Yankee killer, and the guy was so far ahead of his time. He was eating health food, drinking wheat juice – he was crazy. He and I were good friends. We went hunting and fishing a lot and he taught me how to golf. He even owned Bent Oak Golf Course out in Oak Grove for a while. Whatever Larry did, he wanted to be the best, and we needed him to be the best in Game 1.

We had this way of communicating during a game so I'd know what was going on, what pitch was going to be thrown. It was just kind of a sixth sense. He appreciated the way I fielded my position and he'd make pitches trying to coax a guy to hit it to the right side of the infield. I'd call the pick off plays at second and he'd watch my hand and look for one or two fingers or I'd do a circle for an inside move – he

Looks like someone was able to get my signature on that photo of me turning a double play against Keith Moreland in the 1980 World Series. I still think we were a better team than Philadelphia but they really played well that series and we didn't. It would have been tough to think back on the 1980 World Series if we hadn't won a championship in 1985.

was intense and he never lost focus. He made the game fun because he was such a professional. He wasn't overpowering, but he could spot the ball and keep the other team off balance. It was great having a guy like Gura, and following him with a guy like Leonard, who just blew batters away. Dennis could blow batters away, but he also knew how to pitch. All our guys knew how to pitch, they were pros, real pros, and I felt like our staff was going to be the difference maker in this playoff series.

The Yankees scored two runs in the top of the second and we come back and tie it up in the bottom of the inning. We take a 4-2 lead the next inning and that's it – we go on and win it 7-2 against Guidry. By scoring all those early runs we take their bullpen out of the game, and that was huge. And Larry pitches a complete game. I felt like I really contributed in that game with three hits and a couple of RBIs. We're up 1-0 in the series and we can't let them get back in. We had to win the second game at our place to make sure they didn't claim any momentum heading back to New York.

Rudy May is throwing for them in the second game, and we have Dennis Leonard on the mound. We wanted Gura to start the series and we wanted to follow with Leonard because when he took the ball, you knew exactly what you were going to get. He wanted to go nine innings and his mental toughness was on par with Steve Busby, who was one of the toughest competitors I ever played with. Leo always started slow because he didn't like cold weather, but once it warmed up, he was the man. When you have a two-time Cy Young Award winner like Sabes, you can overlook a pitcher like Dennis Leonard, but he was probably the greatest pitcher we had and he was certainly the most underrated. If he wouldn't have blown his knee out, he would be in the Hall of Fame.

I know we're talking about 1980, but when I think of Leo, I think back to a game he pitched in Detroit against the Bird (Mark Fidrych). There were 55,000 people in the stands and I think we won 2-1. The Bird was the biggest thing in baseball, but Leo matched him pitch for pitch. That game had as much electricity as any game I'd played – until Game 3 in New York, and nothing topped that until the 1985 World Series.

We score three runs in the fourth when Darrell Porter and I

singled and Willie hit a two-run triple. U.L. followed with a double and we were up 3-0. They scored a couple in the fifth – Graig Nettles hits an inside-the-park homer; he's the last guy you'd pick to hit an inside the parker. But that's how it went with the Yankees – they always seemed to find a way to beat you. But not tonight!

We go into the ninth and Reggie singles off Leonard to start the inning and you begin to think, *oh, no, not again*. Jim Frey, who replaced Whitey after he got fired in 1979, calls Quiz out of the bullpen. This is Quiz's first playoff action and he was great. He gets Oscar Gamble to pop up to me and then Rick Cerone singles Reggie to second. Talk about white-knuckle – two on, one out. Come on, Quiz!

Quiz was a submarining pitcher whose delivery was like a softball pitcher. He specialized in ground balls, and Nettles was up and he hit a shot to second base. I fielded the ball cleanly and made a spin move to throw the ball to U.L. at short and I don't know what happened, but the ball popped out of my glove. I don't know how I did it, but I managed to grab it in midair, complete the throw, and start the double play to end the game. I went from sheer horror to sheer exuberance in a matter of seconds. For me, the key was never panicking. I could have dropped the ball or thrown it away at second – I kept my cool and let my natural ability take over. All those fundamental drills all those years – they were a big reason I completed that throw to U.L.

We'd won 3-2 – but this wasn't a time to celebrate. We weren't going to celebrate until we had won three games and were headed to the World Series. We knew that just because they were down 0-2 the Yankees weren't going to fold. Everything was in our favor and we were excited, but it was a cautious excitement. We knew the series could turn on one play, but momentum was on our side and we wanted to keep it. I keep thinking about what all my family and friends are telling me – *you gotta do it this time*. And I know all the other guys on the team are hearing the same thing. This was it – up 2-0, playing in Yankee Stadium. These are the games you dream about when you're playing stick ball in the alley behind your house.

When we went to Yankee Stadium for Game 3, we were loose and confident. We weren't overconfident by any means, but we were ready to play. No sleepless night before this game – I was fired up and ready. I don't know if I ever felt better before a big game. Whenever we played in New York, I'd be a stargazer before a game and look and see who was in the stands. You never knew who you were going to see – now it's Seinfeld or Billy Crystal, back then it was Sinatra. They were throwing Tommy John and we had had some success against him. We threw Splitt and it was scoreless through the first four innings. I hit a solo homer in the top of the fifth. Anytime you hit a homer in the playoffs, it's special. But to hit a homer in the playoffs at Yankee Stadium to give your team the lead, that's really special. But a 1-0 lead in Yankee Stadium isn't much, as we found out in the bottom of the next inning. Reggie doubled off Splitt and Frey brought in Quiz. Can you imagine a manager today bringing in his closer in the sixth inning? Like I said, times have changed. Oscar Gamble doubled and Reggie scored on an error by me. I tried to make a play to get Reggie but I made a bad throw and he scores. That was a real down point for me. I made the right decision, but I didn't execute the throw. I'm wondering how that will affect Quiz and the rest of the guys on the team. Man, that was tough, it was hard for me to shake off. Gamble went to third on the play and scored on Rick Cerone's single. But Lou Piniella grounds out to me for the second out and Nettles grounds out to first to end the inning. But they take the lead and you start thinking about another Yankee comeback.

But with one swing of the bat, George Brett made sure that didn't happen. They have the lead and I start thinking about different things between innings – can we beat these guys, can we make a comeback, can we win one and have their fans watch us celebrate? I didn't hate any guy on the Yankees. I know a lot of guys hated Steinbrenner, but he spent a lot of money and built a great team. I did hate their fans – they threw batteries at our guys in the outfield or tomatoes or oranges – I guess they threw anything they could get their hands on.

They say great players rise to the occasion when you really need them and that's what George did for us in the top of the seventh inning. Tommy John was cruising along and had two outs when Willie doubled. They brought in Gossage and I think this is one of the unforgotten moments of the series – with two outs, U.L. gets a single off Gossage – to bring George up to bat. Gossage was so intimidating that he usually came in and got that first batter – but U.L. hung in there and got on base so George could face the most intimidating reliever in baseball.

We have the best hitter in the game against the best reliever and everything just stopped in the dugout. We were all watching George, and I was sneaking a peek at that short porch out in right field. I knew if George made contact, something good was going to happen. When you think of the big home runs in baseball history – Bobby Thomsen's home run off Ralph Branca, Bill Mazeroski's home run to help Pittsburgh beat the Yankees in the World Series, Kirk Gibson's pinch hit World Series homer off Dennis Eckersley or Joe Carter's homer for the Blue Jays – I witnessed a home run as dramatic as any one of those that day in Yankee Stadium. We were all on the top dugout step, watching the best of the best and George connects and the second he hit it, you knew it was gone. I mean, it was way out of there – way, way up in the upper deck. In an instant, a swing of the bat, the crowd went from crazy and noisy to so quiet you could hear a pin drop. We were going crazy in the dugout and as George ran the bases, there wasn't a sound from the stands. It was so sweet. He got back to the dugout with Willie and U.L. and we're pounding them on the back, celebrating, but we knew there was a lot of baseball to be played.

We're up 4-2 and Quiz gets them 1-2-3 in the bottom of the seventh. I don't think they had recovered from what had just happened. We don't score in the eighth and they come back and start another patented Yankee rally in the bottom of the eighth. Bob Watson gets a triple with no outs and Quiz walks Reggie and Oscar Gamble to load the bases. The next batter is Rick Cerone, who had really had a good series and he hits a line drive to U.L. at short. The instant the ball comes off the bat, I head to second and we double off Reggie. They don't score, they have runners on first and third with two outs and Jim Spencer comes to bat. He grounds out to me at second base and Quiz gets out of that jam without allowing a run.

The bottom of the ninth inning was almost anticlimetic as Nettles and Bobby Brown fly out and Willie Randolph takes a called third strike. The most surprising thing to me was Randolph taking that called third strike. Quiz wasn't a strikeout pitcher. He was a ground-ball pitcher, and he retires the side on two fly outs and a K. After that strikeout, I just watched the guys. Willie was jumping around out in left field and the guys were mobbing Quiz on the mound. We'd finally done it. We'd finally beaten the Yankees and we were going to the World Series.

That third game was as intense as any I had ever played. I remember going past second base on the shortstop side to field a ball and throw the runner out at first. U.L. looked at me and asked, "What the hell are you doing over here?" I just wanted it. A lot of people don't remember that it rained some during that game and that worried us, but it didn't have any effect on the game, George's home run, or Quiz's 1-2-3 ninth inning. We finally climbed that mountain and got over to the other side.

"People remember George's home run," Hal McRae said, "but we don't sweep the Yankees without Frank. When Frank first came up, he was a good second baseman with a lot of range. But Frank made himself a great second baseman and a very good hitter. He never got enough credit for his hitting. He put us on the board in that third game, and he made some great defensive plays."

After the game, I found out that I was the winner of the first-ever ALCS MVP Award. I don't remember how I got it. I think they might have given it to me while I was being interviewed, but I really don't remember. And I was shocked to get it. I thought George deserved it for that big homer off Gossage. I was shocked and I was flabbergasted. I know I should remember more about that ceremony, but all I was thinking about was finally beating the Yankees. I do remember filling the trophy with champagne and drinking it, and how champagne stings your eyes – but that was a good sting, one you'd like to experience every season. Oh man, it was a long time coming. I got all caught up in watching the guys celebrate. It was like an elephant had been lifted off our chests and we could breathe again. I don't know what would have happened if we wouldn't have won that series. It was tough losing the first three, but this one might have been devastating.

I think that's why there was so much celebrating going on after the game. We were men who had won a playoff series, but inside we were just a bunch of little boys.

After the game, we wanted to go home and celebrate with our fans, but the club wouldn't let us. The Phillies and Astros were playing in the NLCS and we had to wait in New York to find out who won that series. We were in New York a couple of days, and no one liked that. We wanted to be home with our family and friends. We had finally beaten the Yankees and we had to stay in New York at the hotel and await the outcome of the Phillies-Astros series. I don't remember anything about that time in New York except a lot of room service. We had a lot of security and there weren't any incidents, but it didn't seem

That's one of my favorite pictures. I'm pretty sure it was taken at the 1981 All-Star Game in Cleveland. That was the strike year when they had to move the All-Star Game back to August and it was a complete sellout. I really enjoyed playing in five All-Star Games, especially the ones where my Royals teammates were my all-star teammates.

right to be in New York and not in Kansas City.

We waited, and waited, and waited some more and finally the Phillies beat the Astros 8-7 in 10 innings of Game 5, so we got on a flight to Philly and got ready for our first World Series. It was so great to win the ALCS, but the playoffs are the playoffs and this was the World Series. It was like 1976, 1977, 1978 and 1980 all wrapped up in one big series. We'd reached the top of the playoff mountain and got on the other side. Now, we had to do the same thing in the World Series. But I think we went into the World Series with the wrong attitude. I think a lot of guys were still thinking about the Yankees. I even heard some guys say that that was our World Series – but it wasn't. This was our World Series, and we had to be ready to go physically and mentally.

The series started in Philadelphia and Willie Aikens hits a couple of home runs and we go up 4-0, but they come back and beat us 7-6. Dennis Leonard gave up six runs in a little over three innings and we just didn't play very well. We had the long time off in New York, but

That's me playing second base when the Royals toured Japan following the 1980 World Series. We were over there 28 days and it was a first-class trip all the way. Mrs. K went, representing the Royals, and I got to know what a classy lady she was on the trip. Japan sent a 747 over to take us over to Japan and it was just us and our wives on the flight.

we weren't looking for an excuse, we were looking for a win in Game 2. And we didn't get it. We're up 4-2 going into the bottom of the eighth inning and the Phillies score four runs off Quiz and win the game 6-4. That's two games on the road that we hold leads and we weren't able to keep those leads. We were all ready to get back to Kansas City and hope we could turn this thing around.

If we would have won the series, everyone would still be talking about Game 3. We won it 4-3 in 10 innings when Willie walked, stole second with two outs and scored on Willie Aikens' single. Quiz rebounded from that tough outing in Game 2 and won the game. He pitched 2 1/3 innings and just gave up a couple of hits. We're down two games to one, but we have two more games at Royals Stadium. Willie Aikens would have been the World Series MVP if we would have won it because he had his second two-home run game and we won Game 4 5-3. We scored four runs in the first inning and pretty much held on from there. Leonard won the game and Quiz got the save. It was great how they both kept coming back and playing a big role in our wins. We were really confident going into the fifth game, which was the final game of the series that would be played at Royals Stadium.

We were down 2-1 going into the bottom of the sixth when Amos homered and U.L. hit a sacrifice fly to score the go-ahead run. Gura was pitching and you just had the feeling that this was going to be our game. We'd come home, win three in a row and go back to Philly with the lead. But it didn't happen. They scored two runs off Quiz in the top of the ninth and won 5-3. That was as tough as some of the losses to the Yankees in the playoffs. We had the lead in all three games we lost, but it wasn't over. We still had the chance to rebound in Philadelphia in Game 6.

They had a future Hall of Famer on the mound with Steve Carlton and won the game 4-1. We were never really in it, and that was disappointing. All the games had been so close but they pretty much dominated the final game of the series.

I had a chance to do something in that game when I was up with the bases loaded and (reliever) Tug McGraw throws me a screw ball and I pop it up. Everyone remembers the play where Bob Boone has the ball pop out of his mitt and their first baseman, Pete Rose, makes a diving catch for the out. That's just how the series went for us. Aikens was amazing in the series and Amos and George just crushed the ball, but we couldn't win the close games. I never understood why Frey didn't pitch Splitt. Tug McGraw did a great job out of the bullpen and Carlton won his two starts. Once again, we came up just short in the biggest series of the year. I know a lot of the guys on the team felt the same way as I did, because we didn't want this to be our last opportunity to play in a World Series.

We had some great players on the team, and they all deserved to be World Series champions, but we had to earn it. Now, we're thinking about a World Series the same way we thought about the playoffs after losing all those years to the Yankees. When we came back home, we were wondering what the reception would be like from our fans. We knew it would be good, because it was our first World Series, but we didn't expect a parade. If you throw a parade for a team that loses, what would this town do for a team that wins it all? While I was at the parade, I thought: We have to get another chance and we have to get into another World Series. We have to do it for our fans. The parade was amazing. There were a few moments where I caught myself thinking: It doesn't get any better than this. But then, I realized it could get a lot better. People lined the streets downtown and there was confetti coming out of windows, and all the guys were in convertibles waving to the fans. The fans would come out to our cars and give us hugs and shake our hands. I was so proud to call Kansas City my hometown.

I was soaking it all in, enjoying the parade as much as anyone, but soon after it ended I started talking to the guys and we were wondering what it would take to get us over the hump in a World Series. Just about every guy on the team came up through the system or through a trade and I was wondering if we were ever going to spend some free agent money to bring in some big-time players.

During that golden era of the Royals, we did it all with homegrown talent – we didn't sign a Rich Gossage or Catfish Hunter or Don Baylor or Rod Carew. Mr. K was smart. He knew that we were good enough to compete in our division and he built a club that was perfect for Royals Stadium. We'd reach the playoffs and take our chances against teams that had as much, or even more talent. The Yankees used Sparky Lyle and Gossage as closers and had a setup guy in Ron Davis who would have been a closer on just about any other team in the league. Quiz was a difference maker when he joined the club. I just wish we would have had a few more like him on our roster.

10

"Personally it was a tough time because we weren't making very much money. I had to go to the bank and take out a loan."

TODAY, MAJOR LEAGUE BASEBALL HAS ONE OF THE STRONGEST unions in the country, but it wasn't always like that. That's why we had the 50-day strike back in 1981 – and what a horrible time for our team to go on strike. George was coming off his .390 year where he won the MVP, Willie Wilson led the league in hits and had 100 or more from each side of the plate, Willie Aikens had the amazing World Series and we finally found a way to beat the Yankees in the playoffs. If we had won the World Series against the Phillies, it would have been just about perfect. After the season ended, there was a lot of talk about a possible strike. We kept up to date on it through team meetings, things like that, and none of us wanted it to happen, but we found out that labor disputes were as much a part of that season as balls and strikes. But it was just part of the game where we were making the transition to free agency. The owners and players were reluctant to give up anything and whoever gained ground didn't want to give it back. And from a player's perspective we were trying to gain salary and benefits. A lot of the time it was portrayed as players being greedy and wanting more money, but basically strikes were more about benefits than about salary. So we were able to go through that, and the guys today are better for it. We voted to strike on May 29. They extended the deadline a little bit after our association's unfair labor complaint was heard by the National Labor Relations Board. The owners wanted compensation for losing a free agent to another team. Although some fans were mad at the players – because the season had come to an end – a lot of them supported the players over the owners.

During the strike, I just stayed home and waited for it to all come to an end. You have those fans who are always going to side with management in terms of labor disputes, fans who are always going to think you make too much money, that you should be satisfied with what you got. Then you have to hear people talking about you guys playing a kids game, blah, blah, blah, who have no idea what it takes to play at this level. But I think most of the business people were aware of where we were coming from. And we were coming from a time where if you had a bad year they could cut 20 percent of your salary for the next year. And it is probably still on the books, but they just don't use it. I mean there are countless stories about the guys out of the '40s and '50s and 60's who had very good years and had to play for the same money because they had no power. And I think people realized we were coming into a new age when unions were very strong and prevalent around our country. We got a lot of support from the unions, and slowly, many of the fans joined our side.

I never had anyone come up to me and tell me that they were mad at me. They came up and said they were disappointed, or that they missed the Royals and watching baseball. Mainly they just wanted baseball to come back, hoping we could get things worked out and I think that they realized that one individual player couldn't make the difference. We had our player representatives and we had meetings and they told us what we were fighting for, what we were trying to get, what the owners want to do and what they don't want to do, and you just take a vote to support or not support the strike and go from there. There was a lot of back and forth discussion between our union and the owners until they finally got to the point where smarter heads prevailed and we all came up with a deal.

Personally it was a tough time because we weren't making very much money. I had to go to the bank and take out a loan. Even though I wasn't getting paid, I still had bills to pay. We were all caught in a gray area because we couldn't go out and get a job because we didn't know when we'd have to go back and play baseball. So I just spent a lot of quality time with my family, stuck close to home, did a little fishing and waited and waited and waited for this thing to end. We really didn't have any place to go as a team to work out. It's not like today where there's a baseball academy or indoor sports complex on every corner. I played some catch with Frank, swam, worked out in the back yard, jumped on the trampoline – just did some things so I wasn't sitting around all day. We kept hearing rumors that the strike was coming to an end, and that late July the two sides should reach some kind of an agreement. On July 31, the two sides came together and the strike ended. (*Teams that lost a "premium" free agent could be compensated by drawing from a pool of players left unprotected from all of the clubs rather than just the signing club. Players agree to restricting free agency to players with six or more years of major league service./ CNNSI.com.*) The strike had ended and there were a lot of issues to deal with. The All-Star Game was scheduled for July in Cleveland and they moved it back to August as a kind of preview of the season starting August 10. Attendance dropped and I still have folks come up to me and say, "I never went to another game after that strike." Now they say, "I'm never going to another Royals game after they removed you from the booth." Major League Baseball resumed on August 9 with the All-Star Game in Cleveland's Municipal Stadium. The All-Star Game, which was originally scheduled to be held on July 14, now served as a prelude to play resuming on August 10. Because of the strike, the owners had to figure out a way to salvage the season and send two teams to the postseason. So they decided to split the season into two halves, with the first-place teams from each half in each division (or a wild card team if the same club won both halves) meeting in a best-of-five divisional playoff series. The winners of each mini playoff series would go on to the championship league series. While we were trying to figure all this out, the club fired Jim Frey as manager. Whitey helped develop some really good players in the mid 1970s and then he and Mr. K got into that situation over John Mayberry in 1978. Whitey got fired after the 1979 season. We made additions to the team and we made it to the World Series in 1980. I don't know how many managers are in a World Series one year and lose their job the next, but I bet there aren't many. Dick Howser had just been fired by the Yankees – he was their manager when we swept them in the ALCS and I heard that Steinbrenner took out his anger on Dick, so maybe they looked at it like he was a better fit for the team. Dick managed the last 33 games and we went to the mini playoffs, but lost to the A's out in Oakland. It was a strange season, but we were pleased to get Dick as our manager.

I think he was my favorite of all the guys I played for. When I look back, I had a Hall of Fame manager in Whitey Herzog; Jack McKeon went on and won a World Series with the Florida Marlins and Dick led us to our only world championship. They were all great managers and they each did it their own way. I liked Dick because he was a regular guy. He knew who he was and was comfortable with who he was. He was the first manager who saw my potential as a hitter. Everyone else saw me as a 7-8-9 hitter and Dick saw me as a guy who could produce higher up in the order. In 1983 when George got hurt he moved me into the third spot in the line-up. I thought the man had lost his mind. Then everyone thought he had lost his mind when he batted me fourth in the World Series. He could see more, I think, in my abilities with the bat than any other guy I played for. When he moved me to the third spot in '83, I gained a lot of confidence in myself. I won the team's Player of the Year Award, which I never expected, and I became a more confident all-around player. Dick was used to dealing with veteran players with the Yankees and he treated all of us well, but he especially liked to be around the veteran guys. I hit 17 home runs in 1984, 22 in 1985 and 1986 and 17 in 1987. Everyone knew I was a good second baseman, but Dick saw me as a good baseball player and that really helped my confidence level. He was just such a confident guy to talk to. He made you feel good when you walked out of the room. I was always one of those guys who just wanted straight talk from people, and I got it from him. In spring training, I'd go in his office, ask what he wanted and expected from me, shake his hand and tell him that I would do my best to give it to him. We didn't talk every day – we didn't need to. He brought a winning attitude and approach to the team, and he didn't pay attention to the stereotypes that surrounded me. I was the all-field, no-hit guy and he saw me as an all-around player who could help this team in more ways than with my glove. When he got here in 1981, he wanted to make sure that we finished strong, he wanted to give the fans something to cheer about after the strike. We were averaging around 39,000 a game and we had a love affair with our fans. You had a lot of players back then who weren't making great money and they had to fight more for their benefits and pension and things like that. I was just happy to get 1981 out of the way. We had a good 1982 season as a team. I hit .298 – my best average ever – and Willie Wilson won the batting title on the last day of the season. He edged Robin Yount by one point – I think it was a .332 to .331. He didn't play that last day and that made some people mad, even some of his teammates thought he should have played. That's a crock. He was going after a batting title, and when you go after a batting title, you win it any way you can. If you can win it by sitting, you sit. It was all about numbers and if any guy says he wouldn't win it that way, it's just bull. Robin was a great player and I think a lot of players wanted him to win it just because he was more popular than Willie. Willie made himself into a great hitter, into a switch hitter, into a batting champion. I was happy for him; 1982 was a great year for Willie Wilson.

There are two pretty good athletes in this photo. I'll always think of the times Willie Wilson hit a triple or inside the park home run. He was just amazing. Most guys are gassed when they hit home plate, but not Willie. You needed to put a parachute on his back to slow him down. He was one of the greatest all-around athletes I ever played with.

A lot of people talk about Bo Jackson and what a great athlete he was – and he was amazing. Not many guys can star in Major League Baseball and the NFL. But Willie was a great overall athlete, too. The only thing he lacked was arm strength, but as far as speed and explosiveness, he was something to see. No one could turn it on from first to third like Willie. Most guys are out of gas when they head to the dugout after an inside-the-park home run, but you had to put a parachute on Willie to slow him down. But as far as his power, and his body, and his explosiveness. I think he was in a class by himself. Yeah, looking back, 1982 was a pretty good year, even if we didn't make it to the playoffs. Then, here comes 1983.

We roll into 1983 and we're excited about the season. Then, you start hearing things – word of mouth, rumors – that something weird is going on. And you get to the ball park and the names start coming out and I'm worried about the team. You hear rumors of drug use and selling drugs, things like that. How many guys are involved? At what level are they involved? Do I know the guys who are involved? I knew about the amphetamines in the game, I knew about the marijuana in the game and things like that, but had no clue about the level of cocaine use in the game. So when names started flying around, the first thing I worried about was guilt by association. We'd go on the road and some fan would yell out, "Don't sniff the foul line." They had to get their shots in. We soon found out that Willie Aikens, Willie Wilson, Vida Blue and Jerry Martin were the Royals who were involved. They were my friends, and my teammates, and they were convicted of conspiracy to buy cocaine from undercover federal agents and were sentenced to 90 days in federal prison. That was around the same time Avron Fogelman was trying to buy a part of the team from Mr. K and I'm sure he wondered what he was getting into. I was more concerned about the guys than anything else that season. When Vida came over, we were all excited because he was a great pitcher. I had no idea he was involved with drugs. That was some heavyweight stuff that caught a lot of us off guard. It was all insane, I mean, four of your teammates wind up in jail? We never thought about anything like that happening before the season began. Willie Wilson was the only guy among that group who stayed on with the team. When he came back, we welcomed him with open arms. He's made a mistake – who hasn't made a mistake? He paid for his mistake and it was time to get back to thinking about baseball. I'm not going to be naive and say that his talent didn't play a big role in him coming back, but I think that if you look at a guy's overall body of work and what he has been able to do in his career for the organization, for the team, then it wasn't that hard to see why they brought him back. It was like Darrell Porter when he fought his drug problem. He went someplace, got cleaned up and came back and did a great job with the team. And I think in Willie's case, he was never caught selling or using. He paid his dues, so let's move on.

I never had a personal conversation with Mr. K about that season and all that went on. But I think he was probably embarrassed because you're a proud franchise, you are one of the elite franchises in baseball. And to have something like that happen to you, well, that's tough. It wasn't a Kansas City Royals problem, it was a league problem and we just happened to be part of that problem. So, whenever a scandal like that happens, I think embarrassment would probably be the No. 1 thing we all experienced that year.

I wondered what that offseason would be like, and other than a few people asking about the drug thing, it was pretty normal. My friends and family members knew I wasn't involved in any way. But fans wanted to know who knew about it and if there were any other players who hadn't been caught. It was a small circle of players and they paid for their mistakes. I don't remember seeing those guys hanging out a lot together, but they obviously had some connection. We were wondering what the next year would be like. I know Dick was wondering about 1984. He didn't talk about 1984, he just wanted to make sure we were focused and ready the next year. He was the perfect manager for Willie, because Willie was hyper and high strung and Dick was real low key. He had a way of making people he managed feel comfortable and he and Willie had a good relationship. He was the right guy for the job in 1984, that's for sure. He didn't just have a calming influence on a guy like Willie, he had a calming influence on everyone on the team. I knew he was emotional – and he could get fiery and intense – but most of the time, he was just a guy who kept it all inside and who made the right moves. So as long as you didn't embarrass him, you know, he wouldn't embarrass you. It is funny because so often I think of a team being a reflection of their manager, and I think of the successful Royals as being that. Dick reminds me of a saying that I saw on a wall in Minnesota right before you go out to the dugout. It says: "It's hard to lead the charge if you think you look funny sitting on a horse." So I think that is why he was so valuable - he never changed. And that's why I respect and miss him so much.

After all that happened in 1983, we made a pretty strong comeback in 1984. I don't think that team gets enough credit, probably because we lost three games to none to that great Detroit team in the ALCS. But 1984 was special for a lot of reasons. We knew how to win, and Dick was letting us play our game – great defense, timely hitting and good pitching. And '84 was the year we brought up the great young pitchers – Danny Jackson, Gubie (Mark Gubicza) and Sabes (Bret Saberhagen). We were pretty much a veteran team that was fundamentally sound and our success would depend on our staff. Along with the kids, we had the veterans like Charlie Leibrandt and Bud Black. Charlie was the ol' pro you couldn't rattle and Sabes and Blackie were the California dudes that nothing seemed to bother. D.J. and Gubie were more high strung but as a group, they were all so competitive. Charlie pitched in a lot of tough luck and Blackie was the unsung hero – he wasn't the marquee guy, but you knew what to expect each time he took the mound. We called him Mr. Freeze, because he was so cool. The young guys learned from the older guys and they really paid attention. You knew that any time any one of those guys took the mound, you had a chance of winning the game. You could tell that we were on the verge of something special. We all jumped on the same bandwagon and off we went.

We made it to the ALCS but got swept by the Tigers. They got off to that great start that year and we lost to Milt Wilcox, Jack Morris and Dan Petrie in the playoffs. We thought we'd find a way to win at least one game, but it didn't happen. It was disappointing, but we knew that 1985 could be our year because of the great young talent we had on the mound. When the team added Jim Sundberg behind the plate, to work with the young kids, that proved to be the missing link.

11 "I won't say I was the best offensive second baseman ever, but I will go on the record and say I was the best defensive second basemen ever."

MY DAD HAD A THEORY ABOUT WHY I WAS SUCH A GOOD SECOND baseman. I'm not going to say I totally agree, but you have to admit that it's interesting. He worked in the fields, before there were automatic cotton pickers, and we all used our hands to pick cotton. If you've never had to do that – and I hope no one ever has to do it again – it's one of the worst jobs in the world. You would walk behind the machine and pick all the cotton it missed. Sometimes, the machine would snag and you'd spend all day picking cotton and putting it in these long sacks that you put over your shoulder so you could use both hands to pick the cotton. It was back breaking work, but my dad thought that I was able to develop my ability to field a baseball by the way you had to take the cotton out of its boll. It had really sharp edges, and you had to use your fingers and your thumb to get it out – and you really did develop a method to get it out without getting stuck. I think when my dad said that cotton picking helped me become a good second baseman he just thought he was being smart and funny. But who knows?

Okay, let's talk defense and Gold Gloves. I won't say I was the best offensive second basemen ever, but I will go on the record and say I was the best defensive second basemen ever. I'm talking in terms of range and mobility and the ability to make all the plays. I learned how to play the turf, make the transition from turf to natural grass turn the double play. I think the turf separated a lot of guys when they came in. I just think that was one of the things I was most proud of in my whole baseball career was my ability to play defense. I was a utility guy until 1977, and in my first full season at second base, I won the Gold Glove. I told my dad I wanted to be the best second baseman to ever play the game and I got off to a good start. I wasn't a strong offensive player when I first came up, but I never let my offense affect my defense.

"Frank White saved as many runs as I drove in."

Reggie Jackson
Hall of Fame slugger and member of the 500 Home Run Club

One way I tried to make myself into a great second baseman was by watching the other great fielders. I was challenged by Mark Belanger at Baltimore and John Mayberry on our team. I knew early on that the only way I was going to stay in the starting lineup was for my defense. I knew I could field and I knew that if I had an opportunity to play every day I could break Bobby Grich's string of Gold Gloves. I played a lot in 1976, but Cookie was our starting second baseman. Because I had played a lot of shortstop in the minors, I was still learning the position, and I would watch every second baseman in the league, trying to pick up the little things they did that made them so good. I knew I could catch the ball and throw the ball but turning a double play was the most difficult part for me. It had to do with the way guys slid into the base and the way I wanted to sneak a peek at the base runner – to see where he was – before I threw the ball to first base. I didn't want to mishandle the ball at second base and blow a double play. When I was playing shortstop, everything was in front of me. When you play second, it's to your back and you have to turn to see where the runner is and how close he is to second base. I made 23 errors in 1976 and most of them were from mishandling the ball or making a bad throw. In 1977, Grich went from the Orioles to the Angels and they wanted him to play shortstop, so the bells started going off in my head – this is your time, take advantage of it. After the 1976 season, I went to Puerto Rico to learn more about second base. Defensively, I felt great. Offensively, I knew I had a lot to work on. Plus, I was replacing a very popular player in Cookie and the fans let me know about it. They didn't care if I was the hometown kid, they wanted Cookie at second base and they weren't giving me a chance to show that I could play this game. Then, I realized that I had to prove myself. Nothing is given to you in pro sports, not even if you're the hometown kid trying to make good. There were some tough days. There were a lot of days where people would throw coins on the field when I was running to my position or coming back to the dugouts and there was that one infamous day where I flipped a fan off because I was just so frustrated. I think I was sent to Omaha by the fans five or six times a day. I wound up hitting around .245 that year, but I only made seven errors, won the Gold Glove, and the fans started to appreciate me for my defensive skills.

"Frank White is the best second baseman of his generation or any generation. He was the best. Period."

John Schuerholz
Former Kansas City Royals General Manager

Winning that Gold Glove got me a reprieve from the fans, even some of my toughest critics. People just didn't see me as an everyday guy. I wasn't on the cover of *Sports Illustrated* - I wasn't even drafted. I was from the academy, and people thought the team had to put someone from the academy on the major league club. But I knew that wasn't the case and I knew I was the best second baseman in the American League that season, so I gained some confidence and knew that I had to work on my offense to get everyone off my back. A lot of my friends asked me how I could separate the two – hitting and fielding. I told them that it was easy for me. When it was time to play defense, I didn't think about what I'd done in my previous at bat. And when I came to the plate, all I was thinking about was how I was going to get one base. It all goes back to being a student of the game, learning and implementing your fundamentals. I learned to be an aggressive second baseman. Freddie was a really aggressive shortstop. If a runner came into second base, he knew that Freddie wouldn't hesitate to throw that baseball right through the numbers on his chest. And I developed the same style. I was very fortunate to play with two very strong shortstops in Freddie and U.L. We weren't afraid of a confrontation at second base, and back before they had the rules about sliding into the bag, it could get interesting. If Don Baylor or Dave Winfield were barreling down on you, you have to concentrate on the play, get the ball, and make a good throw to first base. If they saw fear in your eyes, you're in trouble. What really helped me in turning the double play was the feel I had for the game. If the bases were loaded, or if it's first and second and I'm holding a guy on first, I always looked at their cleats to see if they were spikes or turf shoes. Everything was based on the speed of the ball and how fast it got to third, how fast the ball got to shortstop, and that would tell me what technique to use in that situation. Once I developed my techniques, it all came pretty easy.

But that wasn't always the case. Guys like Frank Robinson and Don Baylor and Brian Downing and Kirk Gibson were tough guys. There was a lot of aggressive base running back then – George and Hal were as aggressive as any runners in the league – but those are the guys who stand out in my mind. They were the guys you had to keep your eye on. It's like a batter being tested by a pitcher – like the time Gaylord Perry knocked me down – it's that way at second base, too. You can't let them see any fear, or you're done. It's like a shark tasting blood in the water; if they taste it, they're coming after you. Early on, Whitey called me in the office and said, "If you can't hit or bunt, or play defense you can't play for me." I knew I could get those things done because I learned them in the Academy. We didn't need sports psychologists back then, we just took care of ourselves. You either had it – and if you had it, you could stay a long time – or you didn't have it. This is the highest level of baseball, and only the best of the best make it this far. So you don't need to go out and over-analyze everything. If you have it, you have it – and you're one of the lucky ones who gets to stay and play the game.

"My man Smooth helped me win a lot of games. If the ball was hit to the right side of the infield, it was an out."

Bret Saberhagen
*Two-time Cy Young Award winner
and 1985 World Series MVP*

When I first came up, Big John told me to keep everything simple. He said, "If you make a mistake, admit it and go on. Don't go making any excuses. Winners don't make excuses. And we're winners." And he was right. Guys today have too many crutches. They have too many excuses. Don't over analyze the game or it will drive you crazy.

Frank Robinson was my hero, and he came in hard one time on a double play, and I know he wanted to flip me and see my face planted in the dirt. But it didn't happen. Did he look at me and say, "Nice job, rookie." Are you kidding? That didn't happen back then. The base runners wanted to look around and see the aftermath of the destruction on the base paths. They wanted to see you land on your head. That's what they wanted to see. It wasn't a pat-you-on-the-butt situation; when they went in there, they went in there to let you know

This is a photo that appeared in Rawlings brochures, featuring me and my eight Gold Gloves. Royals photographer Chris Vleisides came over to my home in Lee's Summit and took the photo. It's always been one of my favorite photos.

they were there. It's different today. Back then, a second baseman couldn't even tag a base runner going to second base without getting knocked over. It was just a more physical game. And I miss that part of the game, I really do.

When I got to the big leagues, I learned real quick that this wasn't AAA ball. It was the big leagues with big league players and big league base runners. When Frank Robinson tried to take me out at second, it was a way of welcoming me to the big leagues. Like they told Dorothy in the "Wizard of Oz," "You're not in Kansas anymore." No, you're in the big leagues and you better be ready for anything.

"We called him the Hoover, because he swept up everything that was hit to him."

Dan Quisenberry
Former Royals reliever and Fireman of the Year

There are a lot of ways you're welcomed to the big leagues. And not all of them take place in the batter's box or in the field. One game early my career this guy behind first base was on my case the entire game. I finally got tired of it and flipped him the bird. I wasn't proud of it, but I threw that bird quickly. He was looking right at me, so I hope he saw it. Later in my career, we were in Minnesota one Sunday afternoon and there was this big guy sitting on the front row and he was all over me. I thought to myself, *I can't take this all day.* I didn't know why he picked me, but he was on me from the first inning on. So about the third inning I went up to the clubhouse and I asked the clubhouse kid to go up to the concession stand and buy two beers and two hotdogs and take them to that guy. And tell him they're from me. He got those beers and hot dogs, and he was my friend the rest of the day.

I wish I could tell you how I found out about winning my first Gold Glove. I don't know if I got a phone call from the team or my agent or how I found out. But they used to give you your Gold Glove on Opening Day the following season, and Al Cowens and I both got ours on the same day. That was awesome. We were strong on the right side of our infield and sharing that with Al and my mom and dad and family members was special. It's kind of funny, because my mom and dad didn't know anything about Gold Gloves. They wondered what it was, and I had to explain it to them.

After I won that first Gold Glove, it just made me more determined to win another one in 1978. I think playing with the same shortstop, playing the same first baseman, you don't have to worry about anything but yourself and your game, and I developed techniques and ground rules. I always felt that any ball that hit the ground before it got to the mound I had a chance to catch. So I started watching how the ball came off the bat. If you hit the ball square, it's going to go straight. If you hit it off the top of the ball, it's going to come up higher and learning the turf, you know that on cool days the ball is going to stay down, on hot days it's going to expand and bounce higher. That taught me how in cool weather, you can stay back a little bit, or during hot weather you have to trap it, because if you stay back it's going to make you jump to catch it – it's going to go over

Over an 11-year period, Lou Whitaker – who I'm standing next to – and I won every Gold Glove for second basemen in the American League. I won from 1977 to 1982, he won the next three years, and then I won the next two. I really enjoyed watching Lou play second base. He was a great fielder and a good friend.

your head, and that gives the runner an advantage. You learn how to set ground rules for when runners are going from first to second. If the guy's already off my right shoulder, then I would go to first; if he was off my left shoulder to center body, then I would go to second. I didn't try to do anything extraordinary. I just tried to manage the game, you know just make sure I got the outs that we need to get and then go from there.

"I called him Smooth because he was."

Darrell Porter
Royals all-star catcher

I would anticipate a play before it even happened. If the ball is hit to your right, to your left – right at you – how are you going to react? You have to anticipate a play before it happens. You have to at least play it out in your brain so that when the pitcher pitches, then you'll be able to react the right way. If you have no thought process when the ball is hit, then you're trying to figure it, that brings a lot of hesitation. I always tell my outfielders, if you throw the ball to me, you'll never throw it to the wrong place. And I always made sure my centerfielders knew when I was going to put a pickoff play on second. I'd just turn around and open my hand up on my chest and they'd know it's going to be a pickoff play, so they'd know if there was an overthrow, they'd be ready. The guys in the middle manage the game. You can't manage the game from the bench. You can't manage the two guys out in the middle of the field. You can tell them to move left a little bit, right a little bit but they have to react to what they see. Your guys in the middle have to be thinkers. They have to be loud and they have to be thinkers. And they have to be take-charge type people. There's a trust factor involved, and you always have to be thinking. Playing in the middle of the infield is almost like playing quarterback on a football team. I know a lot of teams don't look at it that way because they are looking at offense first. But if you can get a second baseman with the same range as your shortstop, you got a hell of a middle, and that's what we had with Freddie, U.L. and me.

"What made Frank so special was that he made the tough plays look easy and he made all the easy plays look easy, too."

Hal McRae
Royals designated hitter and former manager

The toughest play for me was backhanding the ball going up the middle and having to redirect it back to first base. I would never jump up and throw. Mine was more of a plant and throw. I'd try to catch the ball off my left foot and when the right foot comes down, just more or less rotate from that side and try to make a play. If you have too much momentum going toward center field you could not make a strong throw to first base. And that little topper that gets past the pitcher, that's a tough play too. But you have a better chance of making that play than the other play.

This is one of my favorite pictures. That's me, Whitey Herzog and Al Cowens after Al and I won our first Gold Gloves in 1977. The photo was taken in the dugout after Al and I received the gloves in a pregame presentation. He was a great right fielder. We had the best outfielders in the game when I played with Al, Amos in center and Willie in left.

Turf was interesting, but you always seemed to get the same bounce, depending on the heat that day. With grass, it could be different at every stadium. The grass at Detroit was real thick and slow. I would always go out early and watch batting practice to see how the balls were reacting to the grass. That way I knew what to expect in the game. At Arlington – and I mean, the old stadium – they had really quick grass. You just had to pay attention to everything around you in a game.

"The best defensive second baseman of all time? That's easy – the man standing next to me."

Ozzie Smith
Hall of Fame shortstop who appeared with Frank White
in Kansas City

After winning my first Gold Glove, I turned my attention to winning a second. There were a lot of good second baseman in the league back then – Willie Randolph, Jim Gantner, Paul Molitor – and I saw it as a challenge to win a second. Many times you hear someone say the first time they win something it's special, but it's even more special the second time they win it. I would challenge myself every series to outplay the second baseman on the other team. Whether it be offense, defense, base runner, whatever it may be, you have to have something to keep you on edge – and that was my edge.

Everything came together in 1978, and I made my first all-star team. George and I were on the team, and I really felt like a complete player. It was fun being on the same team with all the guys you played against, because it gave you an opportunity to get to know them. When your offense and defense come together, I guess that makes you an all-star – at least for one season.

It's unusual to get that type of recognition when you hit as low in the order as I hit. But because I was hitting 7-8-9, I had the opportunity to drive in some big runs. Teams were more willing to give me a chance to beat them than the guys at the top part of the batting order.

You win your second in a row and all of a sudden, you have six Gold Gloves in a row. And that just made me work harder. I watched how the other second basemen played certain hitters, how they turned a double play, and I'd take bits and pieces from the great second baseman and use them to make my game better. I did it every game, every season. I respected all of them, because it was a tough job. The game was on the line every night and your pitchers and your teammates were counting on you to get the job done.

In regards to getting the job done, I only got hurt on one double play, and it happened against Dwight Evans of the Red Sox. It was more my fault than his, but he definitely hit me good. I still had the ball in

The late, great Buck O'Neil once told me that I was the greatest defensive second baseman he had ever seen play. That was perhaps my best compliment, because Buck saw everyone play, including this gentleman, former Negro League star Henry Newton Allen. I have a photo of Allen on the wall of my family room because Buck said he came the closest to me when it came to fielding and range.

my hand, so rather than just getting up (over the runner) and going back, I tried to lean on the ball and hyper-extended my arm. It cost me about 12 to 13 days. But I was never hurt to the point where I had to leave following a double play.

I think there is a fraternity of players today who play the same position, but it wasn't like that in the '70s or '80s. You might kind of talk on the field, talk about field conditions, things like that, but that was all you talked about. Most fields back in those days were better at night than in the daytime. At night they stayed a little moist and the ball stayed down a little better. In the daytime, they dried out a little faster, played a little rougher so you had to be ready for any bounce. I used to pay attention to things like the edge of the grass on the infield you know, is the dirt up near the grass, or is the dirt farther down? So if the dirt's below the grass, there is a tendency for the ball to hit that and go straight down.

When I won the six straight Gold Gloves, I went out and did my best to win a seventh. But it didn't happen. I don't know why – I guess the managers who vote thought Lou Whitaker had a better year. He was a great young second baseman for the Detroit Tigers, and he went on a streak where he won three in a row. I don't know if the managers take it seriously or not. Some do, some don't. I think a lot of it is whether or not they like you – if they like you, they vote for you and they don't care what your numbers are. That's not right, but what can you do? After missing out three years, I came back and won two more – for a total of eight Gold Gloves. The only time I thought I was going to win one was when I was going after my ninth – when I didn't make an error in the field and had only four throwing errors. That was the season I would have passed Mazeroski and to become the first second baseman to win nine Gold Gloves. Maybe they were prejudiced against my age, or thought I didn't have the range I once had. Whatever it was, I was disappointed.

I broke my rule of never thinking I was going to win it – because the first time I thought I had it, I lost it to Harold Reynolds from Seattle (who committed 18 errors). And that was during the time I was hitting up in the order and had the years with 22 home runs. But after I lost it to Reynolds, I was honored by some fans at a luncheon

One of my eight Gold Gloves. These are special. I always wanted to say that I was the best defensive second baseman of my generation and I think that winning eight Gold Gloves helps back that statement. Rawlings does a great job with the award and they are the one piece of memorabilia that everyone wants to see when they come to my home.

where they presented me with their own home-made Gold Glove that looked just like the ones I had won from Rawlings. They were following me and knew that I hadn't made a fielding error all season, and I think they were as disappointed as I was that I didn't get the ninth Gold Glove, so they gave me a special one. It means as much to me – maybe even a little more – than the ones I got from Major League Baseball.

It was one of those luncheons that you don't really believe what's going on. You know it's like, everybody says, "Well, to hell with all the coaches and managers in the American League. They don't know what they are talking about. You played your butt off. You were consistent. And we appreciate that." And I think that's kind of what they were saying. That I'm one of theirs. My fans are pretty passionate fans. Once they locked in on me, as long as I didn't go out and do something totally stupid, they'd stick with me. And I still have that trophy – right on the display area with my other Gold Gloves. It's a great trophy.

The fans kept asking me if I ever talked to Harold about that Gold Glove and I jokingly told him that Gold Glove got him his TV job. Actually, he's very good at what he does. I mean, I think one year, I won a Gold Glove and made 17 errors. It's just all subjective you know – just like me talking about the best defensive players of my era which should be a lot more fun than talking about losing that ninth Golf Glove to Harold. Let's start at catcher and I really liked Darrell Porter behind the plate. He was an aggressive catcher and that made our pitchers more aggressive, too. He wasn't afraid to call an inside pitch when he needed to. Thurman Munson was also very good behind the plate. I think offensively that Carlton Fisk and Johnny Bench were outstanding, but if you want to just talk about pure catching talent, Jim Sundberg would be my No. 1 catcher. At first base, Big John Mayberry saved me a lot of errors with his big ol' soft hands. He was agile and had the ability to scoop up those low throws. Cecil Cooper and Boog Powell were good, too. But defensively, I go with Big John. I always liked the way Lou Whitaker played second. I liked Paul Molitor, too, but he played all over the place and didn't just play second base. Harold Reynolds was good and you have to get Willie Randolph in there, too. But Lou is my first choice. Mark Belanger had range and could do it all at shortstop, then Cal Ripken came along and redefined the position. He had range and a good arm and could hit. He was really the first, big lanky shortstop and now it seems like every good team has a shortstop in the style of Cal Ripken. It was fun watching George become a Gold Glove third baseman, but the best was Brooks Robinson. He played very early in my career and he made plays you couldn't believe. Graig Nettles was a good third baseman but no other guys really stand out or come to mind. Outfield is tough because there are so many guys to choose from. No one could go back and get a ball like Paul Blair, and Amos Otis was a great center fielder. I liked Al Cowens because of his arm, and Dwight Evans was an excellent outfielder. Yaz (Carl Yastrzemski) was one of the best and Fred Lynn, too. I look at those guys and really respect the way they all played the game. I guess because I was always known for my defense, I paid attention to the guys who played with the same passion and enthusiasm that I did. We won a lot of games because of our defense, and that still makes me feel good.

12 "It kind of sneaked up on me because I didn't think about things like that."

WHEN YOU NEAR THE FINISH LINE OF AN 18-YEAR CAREER IN which you played in your hometown and helped bring a world championship to your fans, friends and neighbors, you begin to reflect. There were so many good times – the friendships you made, the two World Series, the 1985 world championship, the eight Gold Gloves – but there were those times where you questioned some decisions and wondered what you could have done to end your time in Royals blue on a more positive note. As I was chasing base hit No. 2,000 in 1990, my career with the Royals was coming to an end. It was probably the worst year of my playing career. It was the year where the organization decided that I was done, so to speak, and some things happened that I didn't appreciate.

It was tough playing for our manager John Wathan, a guy I played alongside during the glory years. I know he was getting a lot of advice from the front office because it seemed like the team was setting traps all season for me to fall into. I was named a team co-captain, along with George, but it seemed like any time I took a problem to John I was labeled a clubhouse lawyer. I thought I was just doing the job a co-captain was supposed to do. But there were other issues, too. I just felt like they wanted me to fall into a trap to make it easier for them to tell me goodbye at the end of the season. I knew it was coming, they knew it was coming and it didn't end like I had hoped. The only good thing about the year was (Royals beat writer) Bob Nightengale, who wrote about me getting close to 2,000 base hits in my career. He wrote a story in the *Kansas City Star* saying I should be given the chance to get 2,000 hits, and after that, it seemed like I got more playing time. I was getting close to (Hall of Fame second baseman Bill) Mazeroski (who had 2, 036 career hits) and I wanted to get as close to him as possible.

I talked to John and asked him about getting more at bats – we were out of the pennant race and I wanted an opportunity for 2,000 hits – but it didn't happen. I know management wanted to see Terry Shumpert at second base and they even put (then third baseman) Kevin Seitzer over there. I thought that from a professional standpoint, they could have extended a professional courtesy to me.

Near the end of the season, we were in Texas when I got base hit No. 1,999. They did extend me the courtesy of sitting me the next game so I would have the chance to hit No. 2,000 at home. I remembered back in 1980 when George was chasing .400 and he got a double to reach the .400 mark. He stood on second base and raised his arms and it was just perfect. I wanted to get a double for my 2,000th hit, and I did. Getting your 2,000th is nothing compared to George chasing .400, but it gave me the opportunity to see the entire stadium. I remember seeing Donna Stewart (the wife of Royals longtime scout) crying, and that really touched me. The fans gave me a great ovation, and it was my last

This is my 2,000th career base hit. For a while, I wasn't sure if I would be able to get it because I didn't play much in 1990. But I was able to get it against Toronto on Sept. 11, at home against former Royals pitcher Frank Wills. It's a special milestone because it proves I was more than just a Gold Glove second baseman.

Photo courtesy of Joe Ledford

one as my playing time was sporadic after that hit. For a guy who was known for his fielding, achieving an offensive milestone like 2,000 base hits was nice. It kind of sneaked up on me because I didn't think about things like that. One day, you're looking at your stats and see you're close to 2,000. And it's like, "Wow, I must have been playing this game for a long time." We had guys like Hal and Willie and Amos and, of course, George, who piled up all the hits and records. But for a guy who came up from the academy and had fans throw pennies and quarters every time I made an out, it was pretty special.

Now, long after my career is over, it's interesting to sit back and look at my entire body of work. That's when I realized that I was a pretty good player who did a lot of good things. I think a lot of it had to do with the fact that I stayed healthy most of the time and was able to get out there and play. You know, it's bittersweet to reach a milestone like that when it comes in your final season and you can see the writing on the wall.

That season was very disappointing, overall, but there were so many good times leading up to it. I think the Dick Howser era was probably the most fun. He saw me as an important part of the offense – I went from 17 homeruns in 1984 to 22 in '85 and '86 to 17 in '87. John moved me back down in the order. I was getting older and I hit eight and then three and then the team decided I was done. I'd played a long time, I knew I was at the end of my career, but you think a career can end on a positive note. Mine didn't.

If they thought I was done, why not come and talk to me and express their feelings about what they expected from me? Instead, they created scenarios that made it easier for them to do what they felt they needed to do – and that was tell me goodbye. I think they assumed I was done, and in their mind, I was done. No one really came to me and said, "Look , you know , we got this young kid and we are thinking that he is able to take over. Will you consider retiring or whatever?" I got nothing like that at all. My 20th wedding anniversary was in October following that season and I talked to (former general manager) Herk Robinson on a Wednesday, I was supposed to leave for Vegas on Thursday and he was saying I needed to come in to talk about next year – blah, blah, blah, blah. And I said, "Well, you know, can we do it on Monday after we get back?" I explained it was my anniversary and he said no we really need to get it done. We were supposed to meet in his office at 7:30 the next morning and he gave me his office number. I got up that morning and I thought about our conversation. He didn't mention my agent, so I figured they must be going in a different direction. I was living in Overland Park at the time and I thought, *I don't want to fight all this traffic to get in there and have them tell me how good I've been to the organization and the community and all that,* so I called Herk on the phone and he told me that the decision to not offer me a contract was decided by John Schuerholz, before he left to go to Atlanta - my tenure with the Royals was done. I said, "Thank you very much. It has been fun," and I hung up. That was it. Herk called me back and Duke (Wathan's nickname) called and I told him them that I didn't need to hear how good I've been to this organization and I didn't need them to tell me how good I've been to the community. I've done what I had to do, it is over, this is the way you guys want to do it, so that is the way it is. I hung up. And I knew that was it – I knew it from the start of the season. They never mentioned a coaching opportunity, a front office opportunity – nothing, not even a ride around the park in a convertible so I could tell the fans goodbye. I thought they might offer me a job as a utility guy, so I could work with Shumpert, or some of the other young guys. It was just a flat disconnect. I know they wanted to develop their own approach to running a team and they got rid of some other guys, like Big John (Mayberry, who was the team's hitting coach). I was bitter. I gave that organization my heart and soul for 18 years. I averaged 147 games a year and I made whatever adjustments I needed to make in the batting order to help the club out. It was a lack of respect that I really had a problem with in the end, you know, because when you lay it on the line, and a team has an opportunity to show you a little respect and you don't get it, it hurts.

That's when (former Royals general manager) Lou Gorman called and asked me if I would consider working for the Red Sox. He had joined their front office and wanted me to be a part of his staff. But I needed to get away from the game and just get it out of my system. I think I only went to one game the next season, and that was when Willie (Wilson) was playing with Oakland. My dad and I went to the game, and that was it. In 1992, I went to Boston. They wanted me to start out in AAA, but I told them I need to start at the bottom and experience everything, so I took a job managing in the Rookie League. I eventually got a job as Boston's first base coach and that was a lot of fun. It was great being with a successful team that played to full stadiums at home and on the road. By the end of 1996, it got too costly working in Boston and having a family back here, so I came back to Kansas City and worked primarily with Blue Cross/Blue Shield. Soon after I moved back, Herk called and we sort of buried the hatchet, and I started doing some marketing stuff for the Royals on the side. When Bob Boone was fired at the all-star break in 1997, Herk called me and asked me if I would consider being a first base coach, and that is how I got back on the field. I didn't have any problem with Herk at all because he said that the decisions made about

That's Toronto's Manny Lee, who was coming over to congratulate me after I got my 2,000th career base hit Sept. 11, 1990 at Royals Stadium. I remember when George got the hit to put him at .400 – it was a double and he stood on second base and saluted the fans. It was a great moment in Royals history. We were losing this game, and wound up losing our ninth in a row– 8-4, but I wanted to tip my cap to the fans to let them know how much I appreciated them.

me were between the manager and John Schuerholz. Herk was just the messenger, and you know the old saying, "Don't kill the messenger." Well, that was how I felt about Herk. He and I have always had a great relationship, and I think it was kind of nice to come back and work at home. When I came here with the Red Sox, a lot of people thought it was uncomfortable for me. I think a lot of people wanted me to come back to the Royals. I got asked if it was weird getting off the elevator in the stadium and making a left turn to go into the visitor's clubhouse instead of making a right turn to go into the Royals. No because I didn't like the Royals. When you are hurt, it's tough. It is hard to get me to a level where I don't like someone. And I try hard to figure out if we can fix this situation. And if we can't, then it's time to move on. So when I move on, you are going to have to convince me that it is worth me doing this because I tried and it didn't work. A lot of those people who were part of all the pain in 1990 were all gone, so it was time to start fresh and be at home and I thought it was a good time to make things right. When I talked to Herk we had a good conversation, and he basically just said that I should be part of this organization, and that is kind of how it went. I didn't want to leave. I wanted to be a Royal for life, but if the organization is not going to offer you anything, what is a guy to do? And we have had a lot of guys who came through the organization who went on to work for other people. And I think that was a common denominator in our organization. We had great players. And I think it would be nice if more attempts were made to integrate former players into the minor league system and coaching staff. This is probably one of the biggest mistakes the club still makes, not utilizing the guys who made team what they were.

When I came back to the Royals, Tony Muser was the manager and he made baseball so much fun. He didn't try to re-invent the game. He didn't try to show people how smart he was. He had a healthy respect for the game and what players should do to be ready to play the game. Unfortunately, I felt we had a team where guys just weren't ready to win. We had guys who had become accustomed to losing, and if somebody came in with a better idea to try to get you to focus more on winning and getting yourself prepared to win, they weren't ready to accept that. And I think, too, the thing that Tony respected was

This is the portrait by John Martin that the Royals gave me when I was inducted into the team Hall of Fame. It's such a great piece of art. John did a lot of art for the Royals over the years, and this one is really special.

Not too sure where this photo was taken, but I look pretty intent on scoring a run.

George (Brett, left) and Seitz (Kevin Seitzer) seem to be having as much fun as I am as they congratulate me after what I'm assuming is a home run. We were so close back then, and moments like this are fun to look back on and share with the fans.

131

It's fun to look back at the old photos, especially my batting photos, because most of the photos I sign for fans are pictures of me fielding or turning a double play. I like that stance – the guy looks like a hitter.

Photo courtesy of Mitchell Layton

This is another one of my favorite photos. The Topps Baseball Card Co., took a lot of its photos in Chicago, and this is a photo of the "the brothers," as Al Hrabosky used to call us, on the team. "The brothers" are, from left, Hal McRae, Al Cowens, me, Al Hrabosky – who called himself a brother – Willie Wilson, U.L. Washington and Amos Otis. There are some real characters – and great players – in that photo.

Willie Randolph, one of the great second basemen of our era, and the legendary Buck O'Neil and I pose for a photo when Willie was a third base coach for the Yankees. This photo was taken when I was working in the front office for the Royals. Willie was part of those great Yankee teams we battled in the late 1970s and early 1980s.

Otis Taylor, the greatest wide receiver in the history of the Chiefs and my favorite all-time Chiefs player, and I worked in marketing and public relations for Blue Cross and Blue Shield for nine years, starting in 1993. It's a real shame that Otis isn't in the Pro Football Hall of Fame, because he was the best. He was so big and strong, and being in the Hall of Fame really means something to him. He's a good friend.

Some people don't like Ozzie Guillen, but Ozzie and I were always good friends. He won a World Series managing the White Sox and was a good player. I'm pretty sure this photo was taken when I was a member of the Royals front office. Whenever you're around Ozzie, you know you're going to have an interesting conversation.

Manny Trillo, who was the second baseman for the World Series champion Philadelphia Phillies in 1980, posed for this photo when I was a member of the Royals broadcast team. Manny and I were teammates in Caracas, Venezuela in 1974. I played shortstop and he played second base. He was a very good second baseman.

This is a special picture. Ron Washington, who led Texas to the last two World Series, and I are visiting with former Royals scouting director Art Stewart. Ron and I were in the Royals Baseball Academy, and Mr. K sent Art down back in 1970 to have him look at the players to see if there was any major league talent. Mr. K was worried that none of the academy players would make it the big leagues, but Art told him there were a few who would.

That's me and former big leaguer Juan Samuel in spring training when I was a coach.

135

Here I am visiting with Hall of Famer Billy Williams, who came with the Cubs as a coach to Kauffman Stadium during inter-league play. He was famous for chewing gum in the on-deck circle and then taking it out of his mouth and hitting it with his bat before he came to the plate. He and Ernie Banks are both "Mr. Cubs," to Chicago fans and it was an honor to get to visit with him.

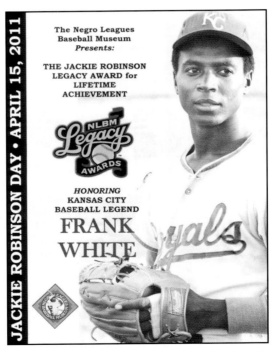

Was I really that young? That photo was taken at the Royals Academy in 1970. It's the cover of the Negro Leagues Baseball Museum program when I won the Jackie Robinson Legacy Award for Lifetime Achievement in 2011. To be associated with Jackie Robinson is special.

I was scared to death when I met Supreme Court Justice Clarence Thomas, center, who was holding the Monarchs jersey with Buck O'Neil. (From left) Buck, Randall Ferguson, the president of the Negro Leagues Baseball Museum; Don Motley, the executive director, Judge Thomas and I all attended an event at the museum, and Judge Thomas took a tour. He went through so much to become a U.S. Supreme Court judge, so I know he appreciated what all the Negro League players went through to try and play in the major leagues.

This photo is from our wedding. Teresa and I partake in the long standing tradition of jumping over the broom from our separate lives, to one life together.

Now, this is what you call a solid gold photo. It was taken during the All-Star Game festivities at the Negro League Baseball Museum when Ozzie Smith and I announced the winners of the Negro League Gold Glove Awards. It was fun sharing the stage with the Wizard of Oz and I will never forget the reception I received from the fans in attendance.

My parents, Frank Sr. and Daisie White, attended the unveiling of my statue at Kauffman Stadium. That was one of the most special moments in my life because my father passed away a few months after that ceremony. I am so proud and honored that he lived long enough to see my statue, because I know it made him proud of me.

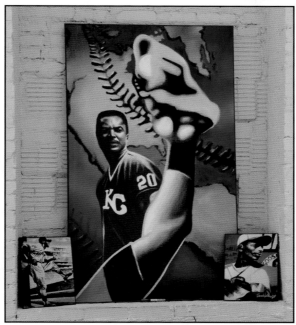

Talk about a hometown kid who made it big - this is a mural created by Alexander Austin, a former homeless shelter resident who has painted some of the most recognizable and popular murals in Kansas City. His work covers the 18,000-square foot walls of Kansas City's Power & Light District. This mural of me was auctioned to raise funds for the City Union Mission - which was once Alexander's home. The smaller murals are of Buck O'Neil, left, and Satchel Paige.

Every time I look out at left field and see the flags that honor past Kansas City Royals division championship, American League championship or World Series championship teams I get nostalgic. Our fans still talk about the glory days and I hope that the guys playing for the Royals today can experience the same kind of success one day.

That is Royals owner, David Glass, my wife, Teresa, and her mother, Mary, at the unveiling of my statue at the stadium. Boy, a lot has changed since 2004. I would have never thought that when they were at the stadium for the unveiling that it would all turn out the way it has.

As I looked out into the audience and saw my parents, my family members, my wife Teresa and her mother, Mary, I thought to myself, "It doesn't get any better than this." And I was right. Most of my days with the Royals leading up to that unveiling where solid gold, but it's funny how gold can lose its luster in such a short period of time.

This photo was take at our wedding in 2000 with some of my sons. (left to right) Darryl, Joseph, me, Jordan, Michael.

I bet you didn't know I was a cowboy. I feel much more comfortable turning a double play than riding a horse, but I was asked to participate in the American Royal and I couldn't resist. I wonder how many fans realize that the name of our team, the Royals, came from Kansas City's association with the American Royal.

What better guy to talk baseball with than Royals Hall of Fame announcer Denny Matthews. Wow, he has seen just about every game the Royals have played and he has called some of my most memorable moments. Denny is the best, and it is always a pleasure to visit with him on, or off the field.

Here I am with T-Bones GM Chris Browne, baseball legend Danny Jackson, and T-Bones bench coach Bill Sobbe.

This is my bobblehead collection. The Royals gave away the one on the left, the Wichita AA team gave away the one in the middle and the T-Bones gave away the one on the right. I think the one on the right looks most like me, but I have to say that one where I'm holding the eight gold gloves is my favorite.

Teresa and I are all smiles while attending a family reunion on Beale Street in Memphis. That photo was taken July of 2012 and there was plenty to smile about as we were surrounded by family members all weekend.

those foul lines. He didn't want anybody to cross that foul line unless they were ready to go to work; he called it the work line. And he didn't like when guys from both teams met up behind second base before the game, hugging and high fiving and stuff like that. So he would make guys run at an angle toward right field away from the other team so you wouldn't see that. He brought back a healthy respect for how guys should prepare to play a game, and from a mental standpoint, what you really need to focus on from the first pitch of the game. But the years he had pitching, he didn't have any offense. Or the years he had offense, he didn't have any pitching or defense. Tony was a hard worker and he had good ideas and knew what it took to win. He just never had the players to be successful.

When Tony left and Tony Pena came in to manage, Muzzy Jackson, who was the assistant general manager at that time, called me up to his suite in Chicago in September and said that he thought that it was time for me to move to the front office so they could groom me in that area. I agreed to do it, and it was probably the worst mistake I ever made. I should have stayed on the field. I was in the front office for two years. I was the special assistant to the general manager, but I never learned that much in the front office. I was more into the minor leagues, going down and assessing the minor league guys and meeting with the managers down there, going over the players. The most fun was probably the winter meetings and watching how that process worked, but I still missed being on the field. It was a 9 to 5 job and I had to come to the office every day, except for the days I spent going to make an evaluation of a minor league team. I had to go to one of the minor league teams, stay for a week and see all five starters. Then I met with the manager, heard his comments on the players and then watched the games to see if those comments match up with what the player was actually doing. It is all an evaluation process for that week. You come back, you write-up a report on each guy, give it to the general manager and that's it.

The Royals knew I wanted to be a manager, and it was interesting how the manager's job in Wichita came up. When I wanted to put my name in the hat for the manager's job Tony Pena got, (general manager) Allard Baird said to go ahead and do it. We met for dinner, talked about some things, and then Monday morning he called me and said, "We decided we are not going to interview you. We feel like you are too valuable to us in the front office." That's when you roll your eyes and say, "Here we go again." Then he told me there was a flight to Philadelphia to interview Tony Pena. They wanted me to fly to Philadelphia, to be a part of the interview with Tony Pena, for the job that I wanted. That was one of the hardest things I ever had to do. I had to put my name in the hat, have it pulled; and then have to interview the guy for the job I wanted. We flew to Tony Pena, interviewed him and then eventually interviewed Buck Showalter, Bucky Dent and John Mizerock. So I was involved in all those interviews. It was tough because you are interviewing guys for a job that I wanted. I thought I was their guy. Then you just have to sit and listen to the process. It wasn't an easy thing to do. I saw what they had me doing in the front office and it wasn't really geared toward preparing me to manage. I had already been a coach for seven years. I managed a rookie ball season, then I also managed a fall league in '95 with the Red Sox and 2004 when I was with the Royals. And even if I hadn't gotten the Royals

John Schuerholz, who built the Royals World Series teams when he was general manager in Kansas City, says hello at a springs training game in Orlando. He was general manager of the Atlanta Braves and I was a coach for the Royals. It's always great to have a conversation with John.

job, I really thought that the right thing to do was to put me in the interview process, you know, give me the interview, let people around baseball know that I was interviewed but that was the one thing I couldn't get from Allard and his staff. When Buddy Bell was hired, I didn't get a phone call at all, which I thought was disrespectful. Finally, when Trey Hillman got the job, (general manager) Dayton Moore did give me an interview. It was a standard interview. I got a second call back while at a luncheon at the Marriott. We thought this was the call. It was a long drive but we made it quick. Teresa waited nervously and excited as I went in. Dayton and Dean Taylor were complimenting me on the interview. They thought I did a good job and then Dayton went on to say, "You obviously know the personnel and you know the financial constraints of the organization, you know the community, you've been great in the community," things like that, but then he said the Royals really felt like they needed to bring in somebody who didn't know the players. I was shocked. And I said, "Well I don't agree but it is your team, do what you have to do." That is when he got on the flight and flew to Japan and hired Trey Hillman. They never really gave me an explanation for their line of thinking. I was getting used to that by now. And after the third year, and the numerous managerial changes we had, and the fact that I wasn't getting interviews or phone calls, I knew this wasn't going to work. So I left Wichita after the 2006 season and started with the Royals in community relations.

I was ready to leave the playing field. I felt like I had done enough with my playing career, with my managing career in the minor leagues along with working in the Arizona fall league a couple times, and double A three years. I really felt that I had done enough to show them I could manage. We had a great 2006 season and I really felt if I wasn't going to get interviewed for the jobs, why keep doing it? So I opted to go into community relations, which allowed me to work from home and do some other things in the community. I worked with the RBI (Reviving Baseball in the Inner-City) Program, went to clinics, some luncheons and dinners, played charity golf tournaments, spoke to a lot of Rotary Clubs and a lot of breakfast clubs. I was mainly just promoting the Royals. I would talk to our general manager, tell him where I'm going to speak and ask what kind of message he wanted me to get out. It was fun to me because it was relaxing. I didn't have to worry about managing and I didn't have to worry about talking about the team on TV and all that other stuff from 2007 to 2010. It was strictly just talking about the Royals in the community, and things like that are very relaxing for me.

13 "Twenty years from now, the kids who play in the RBI Program will know about Frank White and he will never be forgotten."

Thanks to the hard work of some people in Kansas City, Kansas, my #20 will always be remembered.

For years, Inez Holland had dreamed of the moment she was about to experience. She made sure her camera had batteries, and there was a full tank of gas in her car. As she pulled into Eisenhower Field, her lips were trembling and her eyes were misty. The Mission, Kansas, resident was apprehensive at first, wondering what it would be like to meet her childhood idol, Kansas City Royals Hall of Fame second baseman Frank White. Frank was attending an early-morning RBI (Reviving Baseball in the Inner-City) All-Star Game ceremony that featured several hundred youngsters who were participating in the Kansas City, Kansas, wing of the metro-wide program. Holland's husband, brother and brothers in law were coaching a team that included her son. Her son was too young to remember Frank's glory days with the Royals, but Holland vividly recalls being a 9-year-old sitting in the nosebleed section at Royals Stadium watching Frank perform his magic at second base. As she approached Frank, following his talk that seemed to inspire everyone at Eisenhower Field, Holland began to tear up. "I didn't want to get all emotional," she told Frank, who shook her hand and gave her a hug, "but you just mean so much to me. I got your autograph when I was 9, and I will never forget meeting you." That's a reaction Frank often receives, as he has been a fan favorite for nearly four decades. On this special morning, the KCK RBI Program presented him with an honor unlike any he has received. A youngster, who was nominated by his coach on every RBI team, was given the No. 20 – Frank's number that is now retired by the Royals.

"It's like a reverse retirement of Frank's number," explained Cle Ross, the executive director of the KCK RBI Program. "We want every player on every team to know about Frank, to know what he has meant to this community, to know what type of player he was "So, rather than retiring his number, we want to make sure that a deserving young man on every one of our teams wears No. 20. That way, 20 years from now, the kids who play in the RBI Program will know about Frank White and he will never be forgotten." Frank, a resident of Lee's Summit, became involved with the KCK RBI Program shortly after signing on with the Kansas City T-Bones, an independent baseball league team that plays its games in KCK. "Frank didn't know who I was, but I sent him an email and he answered it," Ross said. "I called him and he actually picked up the phone and answered my call. We have 675 kids in our program, and Frank cares about every one of them.

Here I am with 14-year-old Luis Palme, who wears No. 20. He plays for the KCK Royals, a team that took part in the Kansas City, Kan., RBI Program, where every team allowed a player to wear my No. 20. They called it a reverse retirement of a number, because they want every youngster to remember me, which I think it pretty special. This ceremony took place on the Fourth of July and every team in the league will have a youngster wear No. 20.

"For him to come out here on the Fourth of July and participate in our all-star game tells you what kind of man he is. He's special." So special, in fact, that MLB.com was on hand recording the event for a future Internet broadcast. White told the youngsters about his early experiences with baseball and encouraged them to continue playing the game he mastered. "I didn't have a league like the RBI Program provides," Frank said. "I got up early, went to the park, played baseball all day and got home in time to do my chores. I think that kids would be more interested in playing the game if they were given the opportunity, and this program gives you that opportunity."

He praised the number of adults who attended the event. "I see a whole lot of family support here today. That just jumped out at me – how many parents and grandparents are here today. I hope you know how important that is to your kids and grandkids." Luis Palme, a 14-year-old who wears No. 20 for the KCK Royals, met Frank after the eight-time Gold Glove winner took part in a ceremonial first pitch. "This is so special for me," Palme said. "I've never met someone as famous as Frank White. I will always remember this day." Everyone in attendance could probably make the same statement.

"I know I'll never forget today," Frank said. "To know that someone thinks enough of you to make sure that a player on every team will always be wearing No. 20 lets you know that you have made a positive impact in your community. "Now that I'm away from the game, I still want to make an impact, to have a positive impact on players and their families. That's why I was so excited to come out here today and be a part of this event."

"This is a baseball town, and it's always going to be a baseball town."

I hear people say that Kansas City is no longer a baseball town. I disagree. This is a baseball town and it's always going to be a baseball town. When the All-Star Game was in Arizona in 2011, they didn't have enough volunteers to work it. In Kansas City, they had to cut off the number of people volunteering to work the different venues at 2,800. That really pleased Major League Baseball, and it made me

This was a special day for a lot of former Kansas City Royals all-stars. From left, Amos Otis, Willie Wilson, Fred Patek, Hal McRae, John Mayberry, trainer Mickey Cobb and me visit before a T-Bones game during the All-Star Game festivities in Kansas City. Amos and Big John played in the 1973 All-Star Game in Kansas City and every one of those guys was an all-star - Mickey was even an all-star trainer. They were all honored by the T-Bones. It's a shame the Royals didn't do something to honor them at the All-Star Game.

happy because this is my town and I want my town to be a baseball town. People might say I'm at war with the Royals, but I'm not. I'm hurt – really hurt – by what happened. But nothing would make me happier than seeing them succeed. When they were in the playoff race until September a few years back, all anyone was talking about was the Royals. There was a spirit in Kansas City from the early 1970s to the late 1980s that I wish would return to this city. Are the Royals getting close to what we had during that time? No one knows the answer to that question, but the Royals did a great job last year of introducing young players at the right time to get people excited, and attendance went up. September attendance was probably the best it's been in a long time. Now, they have to build on that. You can't lift the fans up and then just drop them. You need to build on one season and follow that season with an even better season. That's what we did back in the early

1970s until we started winning on a regular basis in the mid 1970s all the way through the 1980s.

I think that the people in Kansas City are ready to cheer and be excited. When you have a winning team, everyone prospers. You travel and you tell someone that you're from Kansas City and they start asking you about your baseball or football teams. When Kansas City fans could talk about a world championship team back in 1985, it was amazing. It gives your city a personality, a character that is missing from cities without professional franchises. The Royals and Chiefs have struggled, but I know out in Eastern Jackson County a lot of the fans are talking about a professional hockey team, the Missouri Mavericks. They might not be the Royals or Chiefs, but they connect with their fans, they win and they sell out every game. Their fans love them. Fans just want a team they can support that wins and shows the fans that they care. The Royals used to do that – they did care about their fans, Mr. K. cared about the fans and the players cared about the fans. I think the fans were as special to us as we were to them. For the 1970s and 80s, we were winners. For 10 years or more, the fans could attend a game and know they were going to see George or Willie or Amos or Leonard or Splitt or Sabes. When you see someone play every day, you begin to care about them. You watch them in person, you see them on TV, you read about them in the newspaper and you feel like you know them. And when you know someone, you really care about what happens to them. When they win, you win. When they lose, you feel like you lost a little something along with them. The guys on the 1985 World Series team are as big in Kansas City now as they were back then because we all have such wonderful memories of that team. The Royals need to embrace their past. They need to let the kids of the fans who were watching us play in the 70s and 80s know about our tradition and our success and our heritage. Most of the kids who come up and want an autograph from me today saw me on TV, and that's okay, because I love to hobnob with the fans – both young and old - but they need to know who the players were who really made this club, this organization, so special. If I were still with the Royals, I would recommend that they list every championship season on the back of the scoreboard, so that every driver and passenger in a vehicle on I-70 could see what made this team so special. Teams that don't embrace the past forget about the past, and I don't want that to happen here. The New York Yankees have 27 championship banners waving in the breeze every day. That organization embraces its past, and look how successful the Yankees are. There are young fans who don't even know what we did in the 1970s and 80s. Why wouldn't you want to embrace that? I'd think it would inspire the Hosmers and the Moustakases to want to be a part of something like that. And I think they will – this team has so much great, young talent and all they need is to fit the right pieces together, get some pitching, and we could all celebrate a revival that has been too long in the making.

"You can't take this stuff too seriously. I play baseball. I'm not the President of the United States."

When I finished playing in Kansas City, I kept getting the same question from everyone. They wanted to know if I was going to keep my home here or move on. I never considered moving until the recent incident with me being fired from my TV job, and fans can thank Chris Browne of the T-Bones for keeping me here. But even after thinking about that, I can't imagine not living in Kansas City. In the last five years or so, as the hair on the top of my head has gotten a little bit grayer and it has gotten a little bit harder to get motivated in the morning, I've thought about being a snowbird – leaving when it's cold and coming back when it warms up. I have a home in Arizona that my son lives in, but I just love living here. I love it, I love everything about it. Since I'm no longer spending so much time on the road with the Royals, I'm meeting new people, doing things I'd never thought about doing – having fun, as much as I've ever had.

People are always contacting me, wanting me to get involved in something for kids or charities, and if Teresa and I have the time and think it's a good cause, we'll do it. People always seem surprised when I get back to them – not a manager or an assistant – I get back to them. When my phone rings, I answer it. You can't take this stuff too seriously. I play baseball, I'm not the President of the United States. I'm not the Governor of Missouri. I'm not even the Mayor of Kansas City, I'm a baseball player. I'm not going to stand on some pedestal and look down on my fans, the people I grew up with the inner city, my fellow Kansas Citians. That's not me, that's not how I was raised. If you're going to be standoffish, if you're going to be rude or out of touch, it's going to rub people the wrong way. Suddenly, you turn off one person, then you turn off five people, then you turn off an entire community.

Whenever I see this photo and read the stats – Eight Time Gold Glove Winner, 1980 ALCS MVP and a World Series Champion – I can't believe it. How could that kid who used to walk past Municipal Stadium and touch the brick walls for good luck enjoy so much success in the big leagues? And best of all, I got to share it with everyone in my hometown of Kansas City.

It just keeps going and going and suddenly there is an entire segment of people who aren't going to like you, or remember you – no matter how good you were when you played baseball.

I started playing baseball when I was a young boy, and I never played it so people would like me. Now, it didn't bother me that some girls paid a little more attention to the boys who played sports, but I played the game because I loved it. When you build a following of fans, I think it's important to never do anything to let them down. And when you treat people, especially children, the right away, your name will grow in your community. I think that's where a lot of athletes make a mistake. Some athletes think that all people want is something from them. And that's just not the case. If someone just wants to say hello and get a hand shake or take a picture, I take a moment to do it. Before long, most of them won't even remember who you are, and you'll appreciate the attention. Give them a memory; give them a moment they can remember for a lifetime. Now, I will add that it's up to the fans to pick the right time to approach someone. When you are with your family, when you're at church or out eating or doing some business – that's not the right time, but I realize that most people don't expect to see a baseball player when they're out in public. And they just can't control themselves. Back when I was walking past Municipal Stadium going to or from school, if I saw an A's player I just stood there and looked. I never thought about asking for an autograph. I just watched them get out of their big fancy cars and walk in the stadium and thought to myself, *that's what I want to be when I grow up.* I'd have never approached them or asked for an autograph or a picture or even talked to them. On some days I like to tease my fans a little bit. If someone comes up and says, "I don't want to bother you, but," I'll say, "Then why did you come up here?" They look at me and I laugh, they start laughing and it's all in good fun. I know there are days Teresa wonders why I am talking to so many people, but that's just who I am, that's what I do. I enjoy it – not all the time – but most of the time I really do enjoy the interaction with fans, especially the true fans. And you can tell who they are – you can see it in their eyes. I know players who don't like to be approached by the fans, and that's all right. That's their prerogative, but I can't imagine going out in public and turning down anyone who wants to visit or asks for an autograph. When I'm in the supermarket, I'll notice someone going by with their cart and they kind of look at me – out of the corner of their eye – and they just keep walking. Then I notice them peeking around the corner of an aisle, trying to figure out who I am. That's kind of funny to me, but some guys it really bothers. I guess I just like people. I like being around people, you know. I like talking to people about different things.

Over the years, I had some fans who really stand out in my mind. No. 1 would have to be Top Cat. He was a huge fan who never missed a game. You'd see him or hear him at every game, and those are the type of fans you know really cared about you as a person, not just as a player, but as a person. Sister Marie she was a huge Royals fan. She was a sister at St. Regis and she moved to Minnesota, but she is another fan who makes you smile when you think about her. I think of Santa Claus, Joe – the first fan in line to buy a ticket when right field was all general admission. He looked more like Santa Claus than Santa Claus, and you always had to check to make sure Joe was out sitting in the front row of the right field bleachers. I'd get to the park about 3:00 or 3:30 and he'd be out there sitting in his lawn chair, waiting to buy his tickets. A good friend of mine named Michael told everyone he was my No. 1 fan. Michael passed away a few years ago and you hate to say goodbye to friends and fans. Then there was Curtis, the shoeshine boy who shined shoes down in Westport. I don't know how he did it – but he was there for every game. I think he would shine a lot of the players' shoes from other teams and they'd either give him tickets or pay for a taxi – everyone knew Curtis and Curtis knew everyone. I think he's in Minnesota now, and we used to see him front of the Marriott Hotel, WOW – that brings back some memories. There was Pepsi, who used to dance the polka and wave to Mr. and Mrs. K in the seventh inning and all the Royal Lancers, the folks who sold season tickets for Mr. K. That was another innovation – Mr. K would get Royals fans to sell Royals tickets and they were as much a part of Mr. K's Royals family as the players.

For 18 years I never once thought of playing baseball as a job. It was fun, it was a boys' game and a grown man was being paid to play it. Don't they say you use 62 more muscles in your face to frown than to smile? I guess that's why I like smiling so much. I don't like to frown and I don't like to be around people who frown. It's a cliché, but you can catch more flies with honey than with vinegar, and if you have a positive approach to life, you're going to be rewarded. And oh my goodness, have the fans of Kansas City ever rewarded me. They rewarded me when I played here and they have rewarded me during these tough times by letting me know how much I meant to them – and still mean to them. I always thought that it was easier to smile at someone than look down at them from a pedestal.

I had fun then, and I'm learning how to have fun again today. Cookie Rojas taught me a long, long time ago that when you learn what to do and what not to do, you'll have fun with this game, and that is true. The game defensively came very easy to me; And then offensively, as time went on, I got better and better at the plate. Playing with guys like George and Hal and John and Amos early in my career really made a big difference on how I looked at the game. We were winners. We played to win. But if we didn't, it all ended when the game ended. When it was over, it was over; you didn't carry it home with you, you went to the park and the next day and did everything you could to start a new winning streak. Today, I think too many of the players need special attention; they need people to tell them how good they are. In the time I played, we didn't need any special attention. Maybe that's why the Hall of Fame isn't something that dominates my post-playing career. I get asked about the Hall of Fame all the time, but I honestly don't think about it. It's been such a long time now, I don't think about it and I don't really care about it that much because the people of Kansas City make me feel like I am already in the Hall of Fame. How many players have their number retired, or get a statue? That statue always meant a lot to me, but it meant more to my mother and father. I still see the look of pride in their eyes when I think about the day they unveiled that statue.

"I've seen 'em all – from Jackie (Robinson) to the second basemen who play today, and let me tell you this, Frank White was the best second baseman I ever saw. He defined the game on turf, had more range than

anyone and hit cleanup in the World Series. Is Frank White a Hall of Famer? You bet he is."

Buck O'Neil
Baseball ambassador and former Negro League great

It's special to me that people still think about me going into the Hall of Fame. But what would it mean to go into the Hall of Fame? My life wouldn't really change; but in a small way, it might change the lives of people who care about me. If I am ever elected to the Hall of Fame, it will be a special honor for me but it will also be for the people of Kansas City; the fans who want to see it happen, the people who shake my hand, look me in the eye and say, "You should be in the Hall of Fame." Those are the people I want to share it with. I've had some interesting Hall of Fame discussions with fans; I think they are more passionate about it than I am, especially in the inner-city. I like to go everywhere in this city, because it's where I grew up and call home. I might go someplace and surprise people to find me there – but it's just home to me. I grew up in the city and still have family there. I have a house I rent to my brother-in-law and I still go down there to see family members. My older brother Vernon lives in my mom's old house – which burned, and was rebuilt. I bought the house next door and remodeled it and my sister lives across the street. It's where I grew up, it's where my family was and still is today. I hang out, visit with friends, mow the grass, have fun. And I've never had anyone ask, "Frank, what are you doing down here?" Because they know when I'm down there with them, I'm with family and friends. Old friends come by, they see me mowing the yard or working on the house and they chit chat and have a beer or whatever. We just talk, and go about our business. No big deal – never was, never will be – it's just home.

"I remember sitting between him and Whitey on the bench in San Diego and listening to them talk about stuff. That was pretty nice, I enjoyed that."

With the All-Star Game being in Kansas City this summer, there has been a lot of talk about past All-Star Games. To be honest with you, I don't remember much about my first All-Star Game. It was in San Diego in 1978, and I remember there were quite a few Royals players there – George and Freddie started, but at the all-Star Game Darrell and I were reserves – and I remember getting this really nice oil portrait that all the first-time all-stars got. I have it hanging in my home. Tommy McDonald (a pro football Hall of Famer) painted it, and I was really surprised to get something that nice. We lost the game, but it was so much fun being around the stars of the game. Like I've said before, we didn't fraternize much back then, but at the All-Star game you could talk to the guys you played against and you could talk to the National League players you never saw. Billy Martin was the American League manager. I always admired Billy. Like him or hate him – and there were a lot of Royals fans who really didn't like Billy – he knew the game. With Billy, there were a lot of off-the-field things that always seemed to happen with him, but he knew the game. He never missed a detail, never was out-managed, and he always had that ability to get his team an edge with the umpire; he knew every trick in the book. I remember sitting between him and Whitey on the bench in San Diego and listening to them talk about stuff. That was pretty nice, I enjoyed that. They talked about their Yankee experiences – a lot of people might not know that Whitey played for the Yankees – and they talked about baseball. I could talk about baseball, or listen to someone talk about baseball all day. They talked about winning – and they were winners. We lost the game 7-3, but it was still fun. It was fun, but I remember every guy there had an edge. To be the best at what you do, you have to have a little bit of an edge. And you have to have an ego – and there were a lot of egos at those All-Star Games. I'm not saying that in a bad way. The best players were there, there were a lot of egos and you were there to win. And we didn't win many of those games. I think the one thing I really wanted to do at every All-Star Game was watch those guys go about their business. See what made them tick. See what made them the best, what made them all-stars. You can laugh, you can have fun, but you're there to win. We talked about doing whatever it would take to win a game – taking a guy out at second, having a pitcher throw an extra inning, keeping some of the key starters in the game. You had fun, but it wasn't as much fun if you didn't win. Surprisingly, we had a good chemistry in the clubhouse. We were a team, even though we were just together a few days. There was a diverse group of players in there and they were the best. Some had come from championship teams, and those were the guys I really paid attention to. I remember wondering how the A's won three consecutive world championships when all they seemed to do was fight with each other in the clubhouse. They might have fought with each other in the clubhouse, but once they got on the field they fought to win the game. That team could've played without a manager because they knew what it took to win. And they had the great players. And once the Royals got some seasoned players – the young guys who all grew up together – we learned what it took to win. We didn't fight in the clubhouse, but we developed an approach to winning and it worked for more than 10 years. All we had to do was take care of our business, because we knew everyone else was going to take care of their business. Back then, the team brought us up when they thought we were ready to play, when we could handle the pressure and get the job done. Today, they seem to rush the kids up, and look at the results. These young kids are trying to figure things out, and sometimes it just doesn't work. And it's not a young kid's fault to reach this level and struggle. Back in the day, George struggled, I struggled and a lot of other guys struggled and we were we sent back down to the minors.

When you struggle, get sent down, come back and become an all-star it's even more special. Back in 1977, when I won my first Gold Glove, I knew that Bobby Grich – who was a Gold Glove second baseman for Baltimore – was going to California and was going to play shortstop. I knew that might open the door for a Gold Glove and eventually, a spot on the all-star team. I made my first all-star team in 1978 and really wanted to make it again –and I did the next year, in Seattle. I won another Gold Glove and wound up winning six in a row. But the All-Star Games weren't quite as frequent. I had to work hard and was lucky to play for a winning team that got a lot of attention. But I have to admit, there were times when I was sitting on an all-star bench and looking at the guys around me, and I had to wonder how a kid from the Academy was there at an All-Star Game. Coming from where I came from to get to that point in my career was pretty phenomenal. That's why it's so important for me to go back into the community and talk to kids to let them hear my story, to inspire them and to help them realize that dreams do come true. If you chase after a dream sometimes you catch it. I went on and made all-star rosters in 1981, 1982 and 1986. We lost in 1979 in Seattle, 7-6, we lost 5-4 in Cleveland in 1981 – the year they moved the game back to August because of the strike – and in 1982 we lost 4-1 in Montreal. I never got an all-star hit until 1986, and it's one of the biggest hits of my career because it was for Dick (Howser).

"My first all-star hit was a homer – and it was for Dick."

My first all-star hit was a homer – and it was for Dick. When you win a World Series, the manager from each team manages the All-Star Game the next year, so Dick was going to manage the American League and Whitey was going to manage the National League team. I had never gotten a hit in an All-Star Game – I was a reserve or a pinch runner – and I wanted to get a hit in this game because we all wanted to win it for Dick. He was just at the point where the cancer was starting to affect him. You wouldn't notice is all the time, but there were a couple of times he called me Lou (Whitaker, the Detroit Tigers second baseman) in the dugout. You don't think much about it at first, then you realize what's happening down the road when you find out about his health issues. We're up 2-0 on a Lou Whitaker home run and Whitey brings in Mike Scott, a nasty pitcher with the Houston Astros. Cal (Ripken) and Jesse Barfield struck out and I'm thinking, that I don't want this guy to strike out the side. Dick sends me in to pinch hit for Lou Whitaker, and before you know, it I'm down 0-2 in the count. He was throwing a split-finger fastball and I'm looking to make contact. He throws me a fastball and I hit it for a home run. My first all-star hit was a homer – and it was for Dick. I was so happy running around the bases. It looked like we were finally going to win my first All-Star Game and I was going to be able to share it with Dick and George. Dick was so happy after we won. It was special for him, even though he wasn't himself because of his cancer. During the game, and at the postgame news conference, he could recognize players, but he would call them by the wrong name. He said he wasn't feeling well, but we had no idea how bad it all was. But the smile on his face when we won that game 3-2 was something I will always remember. It wasn't as big as beating Toronto in the ALCS or the Cardinals in the World Series, but I just respected him so much and loved him so much as a manager. I was thrilled to play a role in him getting that win. Back then, the National League pretty much dominated the American League, so it was big to get an all-star victory.

Looking back on all my all-star appearances, I remember how there were always other Royals players at the games. In Montreal, in 1982, we had five players and Mickey Cobb was the trainer and Dick was a coach. I think George, Hal, Willie and Quiz all made it so we had seven people representing the Royals. That's why I always cringe when I hear someone talk about the Royals' problems and small-market teams. We were a small-market team in 1982 and had seven people at the All-Star Game. If you draft good people and do your job, you should win. Mr. K never sat around and complained about the Yankees and their payroll. He didn't complain about what the Red Sox were spending. He knew we only played them a limited number of times during the regular season and that all he needed to do was build a team that could compete and win the division. Then, in a short series, anything can happen. Once you get in the playoffs, it's a crap-shoot anyway. He spent the money he felt he needed to spend to compete in the regular season. He allowed us to have a window of opportunity that lasted from the mid 1970s to the mid 1980s, where every year we competed for a division championship and were lucky enough – and good enough – to appear in two World Series.

14

"I was shaving and looking at myself in the mirror and I didn't like myself anymore. I didn't like who I was seeing."

I CAN'T REALLY PUT A FINGER ON WHEN EVERYTHING BEGAN unraveling, but back in 2007, the Royals had their own network, RSTN (Royals Satellite Television Network). Neal Harwell and Kevin Shank were in charge and they asked me to do a couple of games in Omaha (the site of the Royals AAA club). I did those games with Dave Armstrong, and they were a lot of fun. And then, in 2009, when (Royals Hall of Fame pitcher and broadcaster) Paul Splittorff wanted to cut back on his schedule so they asked me to do some games. So I did 28 games in '09, and I also did the pre and post game shows. Then in 2010, I was going to do 40 games, plus pre and post game, but that's when Paul had his health issues on Opening Day. They asked me to fly to Chicago for a series with the White Sox. I think I ended up doing 135 games and it took off from there. While this was going on, I still had my job in community relations. I was doing probably 60 or 65 appearances before I started doing the TV. Then when I started doing TV, it got down to around 40, 45 – it went from doing a lot of things every day to the more high-profile appearances. But I still was doing apperances at the stadium at the Royal's request. There were days I'd do the open for the broadcast, visit a suite and wouldn't have enough time to eat dinner. I'm doing all this along with broadcasting the games, and the Royals told me they couldn't use me as much as in the past because of my broadcast duties. I first heard from Toby Cook (vice president-community affairs & publicity); and the guy he reported to was Kevin Uhlich (senior vice president-business operations). This all started in the spring of 2010. They wanted to cut my salary on the community relations side. I was making $150,000

for the community relations job and $1,750 a game with Fox Sports. I
met with (team president) Dan Glass in spring training and I told him
that it didn't make sense to me to cut my community relations salary
because I considered that my job. I considered that a job I was going to
retire from. So they left me alone the rest of that summer. Then, in the
fall of 2010, Toby, Kevin and I met at the Hereford House. They told
me again they were going to cut my salary from $150,000 to $50,000. I
told them that they were not going to get all the benefits of my services,
because I was doing everything for the club, from making appearances
to handing out t-shirts on Fan Appreciation Day. After that meeting,
I told them that I needed some time to think about things. I had not
had a raise since 2008. I never complained about anything, then all of
a sudden, a whole bunch of stuff started rushing through my head, like
the interviews I didn't get, how I never complained, how I always took
the high road, how I was always the positive guy. It was Dec. 3rd. I was
shaving and I looked at myself in the mirror and I didn't like myself
anymore. I didn't like who I was seeing. I saw a guy who reminded me
of that cereal commercial that was on TV when my kids were going
up, "Let Mikey try it," anything that people wanted to try, let Mikey
try it first. And Mikey never complained. So I felt like that guy. I
was Mikey. And I just felt like I had really busted my butt for this
organization over the last 15 years and I thought I had done everything
they wanted me to do, when they wanted me to do it, without
complaining. When they came to me with that cut in salary, it was all
about taking me for granted . And I didn't want to be that guy, I didn't
want to be that guy everybody says, "Oh he is just happy to be around,
we are just going to appease him." I really thought I was doing genuine
work. And I think that when I looked at myself that day, I said, "When
are you going to stand up and be a man? When are you going to tell
these people that what they are doing is not right?" I called Teresa into
the room and I said, "Sweetie, I got some bad news for you," and she
said, "What are you thinking," and I said well, "I just don't like myself
anymore." I've always taken the high road, I've never complained, I've
been away from you so many times doing things that didn't make sense
but I did them, and I just can't do it anymore. I told her that we may
have to sell everything we've got but I can't work for them anymore.

And she said, "If that's how you feel, I'll support you." I don't know where this TV thing is going. I told Toby Cook, "You guys haven't offered me the TV job on a permanent basis." I also said, "To me the community relations job is my real job." I said, "If you guys just leave me alone for the next three or four years, I am not going to complain about the salary. I'll just retire and move on." The organization response was, "We are not going to do that." So everything I asked for I never got. I just reached that point where, when I made the personal decision to resign, it helped me both physically and mentally. My health was starting to suffer because you can only hold stuff in so long and I really thought if I just didn't make that move that I would, well, I would make a scene somewhere, and I didn't want to do that.
So I thought the best thing for me to do was resign as a Royals' employee.

I e-mailed Toby and that as of December 31st, I would no longer be a Royals' employee. I got no firm response from that. Then December 31st rolled around and I still got no response. It's the end

That's a photo card Fox Sports made up for me to hand out and sign for my fans when I was in the broadcast booth for the Royals. The way things came to an end with Fox and the Royals, I'm betting those cards are going to be real collector's items.

of the year. What are they waiting on? So a few days later we started exchanging e-mails and I wasn't really that concerned because I knew I had at least another year on TV. I went in talked with Tom Pfannenstiel in human relations about everything that was happening because I was concerned about my pension. All I wanted to do was get the last three years in, get my pension and then whatever happens, happens. So I told the Royals I would work for $50,000, but I wanted to do it as a contract employee and not a Royals employee because of pension concerns. Toby and I hammered out 25 appearances and I thought that was it – but Kevin Uhlich kept coming back with more stuff – for the same $50,000. So I'm thinking, *you guys are telling people that you are not using me as much as you want and that is why you are trying to cut my salary.* Now I'm trying to work for this amount of money, but the organization continues to make it difficult and we are trying to do more high profile stuff. So Toby and I, remember this is all through e-mails, keep trying to figure this out. Uhlich kept coming back with more demands, so finally the last time he came back to me, he said well, we want you to sell suites in the off season. Suites in the off season? I said, "Guys, I don't sell suites in the off season. I have no clue how to sell suites in the off season." Even though I would have possibly made more money, I had no clue how to sell suites. That was the last straw and it was the final. We are down to around the middle of January by then and on January 17th, I e-mailed my resignation into Human Resources, and I got no response. I did an appearance at Fan Fest, I did a caravan (where Royals players visit surrounding communities). And then it was somewhere around the 26th or 27th of January I was at the Whatsoever Community center doing a function, and Dick Kaegel (who covers the Royals for MLB.com) was there, and said he heard there had been some changes. And I said, "Yeah, but you need to talk to those guys first." So Dick talked to Kevin Uhlich, and then he came back to me and asked what I wanted to say. I told him, "What I want to say, you don't want to write." So we took the high road again. All I said about this whole thing was that I enjoyed my time as manager, coach, front office personnel – all that stuff. I wish we could have worked something out but it was time to move on and concentrate on my broadcasting career, and that is kind of how we left it. The Royals accused me of leaking this story to the press when it was Kevin Uhlich talking to Dick Kaegel.

When it got out that I resigned, the Royals took a pretty good beating on the local radio shows, but I had no control over what the fans were saying. The Glass family was being criticized, but I couldn't stop the fans from saying what they were saying. That was out of my control. Maybe they realized, like I had realized, I was being taken for granted. I know I made a difference in people's lives because people would tell me that. I had no clue what type of job I was doing on the broadcast. No one with the Royals or Fox ever told me anything bad, but when I talked to the fans they would tell me that they were learning things from me every night on the broadcast. That's when I realized I was doing a good job. I even called 810 and 610 radio the same day the story came out and to inform them I had verbally resigned and not been fired by the Royals. I was trying to ease the verbal assault on the Glass family because a series of events occured that was not in my best interest.

15 "I'm not the problem."

THROUGHOUT THIS ORDEAL, THE ONE GUY I NEVER TALKED WITH was the one guy I needed to talk to, and that's Dan Glass. I finally had a conversation with him and he said that I had done irrevocable damage to the organization and he didn't think it could be repaired. And my comment to him was, "that wasn't my intention." I told him, "I'm not the problem." The problem was with his people. I asked if he knew what had happened – all the details – and he said he knew. I told him "I think you guys have done irrevocable damage to me." I told everyone I resigned. I didn't put anything back on the Royals. I even went on 610 and 810 call-in shows to say I was not fired and that I had resigned. I was just trying to keep things normal. I was jumping through their hoops, I couldn't get an answer from anyone, and right then I knew that 2011 was going to be my last year on TV. I even went home that night and told Teresa, "This is our last year on TV." I know how people think. When Dan made that comment to me, it was like okay, you can't have a guy resign and take his TV job away in the same year. So I knew what was going to happen when that season was over.

I remember e-mailing my boss at Fox in September, saying, "Look I don't have a good feeling about this job next year, so if you guys decide you are not going to bring me back I would appreciate you letting me know by the end of September. That way I will be able to get out and find a coaching job or something like that. But, they waited until December 3rd, when all the coaching and television jobs are filled. Why wait that long? Just another insult, even though I believe that was the date my contract officially ended. The Royals could say I was super critical of the team, because I assumed it was going to be my last season and because of the conversation I had with Dan Glass and people at Fox. Jack Donovan, the Fox Sports Midwest general manager, came to town and I met him on the Plaza. He told me the Royals wanted to go in a different direction – no real reason was given at that moment. They wanted to take a different direction. I also found out that our producer, Kevin Shank, was also being let go from his duties – and he had done a great job, in my opinion. I kept pushing him, I said, "Jack, the ratings were up this year. I got no complaints from the fans, you guys, no complaints from the Royals. I got no complaints from the players, their families – so where is this all coming from?" I knew in the back of my mind where it was coming from. I just wanted him to say it. I waited, and waited, and finally he said that the organization thought I was too negative. I said, "Really? So where did that come from?" And I never got an answer.

I knew I wasn't the problem in the broadcast booth, but the organization wanted me to be the problem – so my contract was not renewed by Fox. I don't like to assume, but I have to think that Dan Glass made the final call. And I think it was because of me quitting the community relations job, and the team getting so much bad publicity. I think he took it personal. Someone high up in the organization let Fox know they were unhappy. Who else could it be? I went from my $150,000 community relations job to an offer of $50,000. They wanted me to do more games, but said the games cut into what I was doing in the front office with the community relations job – so we kept trying to come up with a compromise and it never happened. I had to laugh because it was like a tug of war that was going nowhere – like that tug of war with the Dallas Cowboys at the 1978 Battle of the Network Stars that lasted 78 minutes. We had three or four inches of the handkerchief on our side and Keith Jackson said it's a tie. That's how I felt – like a tug of war that was never going to end.

Some of my friends have asked me if I felt like I entered the broadcast booth with a chip on my shoulder because of all the stuff that happened to me before the season started. Absolutely not! I think I did a great job. We were broadcasting games for a team that wasn't very good and Ryan (Lefebvre) and I always did our best to make it positive, and if we ever got too critical, Kevin was always in my ear saying, "Let's move off of this subject." The decision to not renew my contract had nothing to do with the broadcasts. It was all personal and it all involved me and the front office. I think Ryan and I had a great relationship. I thought the broadcasts went well. I had too many good comments from the parents of the kids who were playing for me to believe the broadcasts were negative. Yes, I was a broadcaster, but I also felt like a coach in the booth. I don't know if they have a coach in the booth now, someone who can tell the fans what to watch out for, but I think the broadcast team now is more critical than when Ryan and I were broadcasting the games. I was in a no-win situation. Regardless of how well I did, I was gone at the end of the season. People aren't big enough to appreciate a job well done, because of some other incident that won't allow them to be objective. Someone wanted to flex their muscles, and when they did, I was let go.

We celebrate as a family at my Mom's 80th birthday!

It still bothers me that I don't know who made the final call. All I could ever get was "the Royals," when I asked about who made the call to Fox to have Jack Donovan not renew my contract. It just got too personal for someone. If it was Dan, that will really bother me, because at one time we had a good relationship. I was one of the staff members who befriended him and we talked quite a bit about baseball. I made it a point of going down and talking with him. I thought maybe I could offer a little advice, make him feel a little bit more comfortable. He's a likeable guy, fun to be around. When I was managing in Wichita he would come down and we'd spend some time talking about the team. We would work out, go to lunch, those types of things. I always thought we had a good relationship. I thought we were friends. Then it all just sort of turned when I started doing more games for Fox. I've talked about money so much, but that's what rules the game today – money! Someone, and I guess we'll never know if it was Dan, was unhappy that the team received negative publicity when I resigned and they decided to take it out on me in the booth. As it turned out, I lost a year round job with my resignation and then got removed from the booth. They just didn't see the value in having me as a part of the Royals family, and that still bothers me. It bothers me a lot. They never really acknowledged it or showed their appreciation in terms of comments, actions or loyalty.

"You'll never see me in that stadium again."

To this day, I haven't talked with anyone from the Royals. It all started with them wanting to cut my salary, even though I was doing a good job in the community relations department. I resigned when they kept adding things for me to do. Then, when I tried to talk to them about why I was removed from the TV job, everyone just backed off. I keep looking back, wondering if I could have done anything differently. I mean, the Royals were my family. The only thing I look back on – and it's one of my biggest disappointments – is that those guys over there never really got to know me.

When the Royals unveiled my statue in 1995, it was a special moment for me because I got to share it with my late mom and dad. The statue was originally on the southeast corner outside of Kauffman Stadium before they moved it inside to the center field fan area. I wonder if I'll ever see it again?

"That was a tough time for both of us," Teresa said. "I can tell when something is brewing in his mind; it's like the wheels are turning, and he won't verbalize it initially. But when he makes a decision – especially a decision like that – it has to be his."

I always made a point of knowing the people I worked with. I'm just that kind of guy – I like a work environment where everyone knows each other and gets along. They never really took the time to get to know me. I know they got good comments, letters and e-mails – but they made no effort to tell me about the good things I was doing. They never said, "Let's go to lunch. Let's go to dinner with our wives." There was nothing like that at all. And I think if they would have taken the time to do that, they would have found out that I'm all right. And I think they would also realize that a lot of the decisions they made were based on assumptions. Someone would assume this about me, and make a decision without asking me about it. That's why I would never come out and say Dan was the man responsible for FOX not renewing my contract because I don't know if that is true. I'd hear or read comments from the organization saying that I didn't think Ned Yost was a good manager or that I was trying to undermine Ned and his staff. That's not true! If that was true, why didn't someone come to me and talk about it? Why? Because it wasn't true. I worked hard at my job, but I also worked hard to stay out of people's way. They don't know how I feel about that team. My love for this game and this organization is stronger than anyone could ever imagine because when you are part of something as special as the Kansas City Royals – especially when you were a kid from the inner city who dreamed of playing for the hometown team – you have a strong love for that organization forever.

We brought an expansion team to the World Series. We – the players, the coaches, the managers, the front office, the ownership group – we did that. It hurt me when had out first 100-loss season. It hurt me when we finished in last place for the first time in team history. And it hurt me when our organization went under .500 for the first time in team history. And it definitely hurt me when we lost 100 games in a single season and some of our key players didn't play in that game to avoid the embarrassment of 100 losses. We have people in the organization who talk about winning, but do they really know what they're talking about? They don't know what it took to turn this team into a winning team and then taking that winning team and turning it into a championship team. They can't draw from the same history I could draw from. We don't want any credit for what we did when we played, but we think we could be beneficial to the young guys who are playing today, because we were there where they are today, and we could talk to them about winning and what it takes to succeed. I think you have to embrace your past to have a successful future. I think the young kids today would enjoy talking to the veteran guys who got it done. They need guys to talk to the guys on a team that is struggling. We all went through it and we survived the rough spots and enjoyed the success that followed. I think a lot of the teams miss the boat because they don't recognize the value that is right there, staring them in the face. I think that that is why the radio stations use the former players, so they can get the opinion of a man who was on the field, who got it done and who can talk about the game today. I think a team like the Royals needs to embrace its past, but I was a part of that past and you saw what happened with me. I'll never be a part of that organization again. You'll never see me in that stadium again.

"I think they just wanted to control what I was doing."

I've never talked to anyone about this, but I don't think the Royals totally wanted to get me out. I think they just wanted to control what I was doing, and I think they wanted me to be a part of the organization where the situation was more beneficial to the team than it was to me. I was thinking a lot about my pension, and I wanted to retire when I was 65 or 66. I wanted to be able to leave on my own terms. If we could have worked something out where I could have been a part of the front office for three or four more years – even at a cut in pay – that would have been beneficial for both sides. I could have worked until I retired, and they wouldn't have received all this negative publicity. I was a lifelong member of the Royals and all of a sudden I have people making judgments on me who didn't know me. I hadn't received a raise since 2008. I only had one performance evaluation in three years – it was like they just didn't care. And I could have stayed in that community relations job and dealt with everything, but I would still be the guy who had high blood pressure and who was miserable and didn't like himself.

"The last year or so was so tough on Frank, it really took its toll," Teresa said. "But this last time around, it was different. He just couldn't take it anymore. And I couldn't watch him go through it anymore. I told him to do what he felt was best for himself and his family. The most important thing to me was his health. You can't take all those things and continue to push them aside and try to make things the way you want them to be. He tried to make them work out, but in the end, he made the right decision. I've seen him go from tense and worried to more relaxed, more open. It's better – but the hurt is still there. But he feels like he is at a new point in his life where he is doing new things and meeting new people and enjoying himself more than he thought possible."

I could have easily been that guy with high blood pressure and miserable every day going to a ball park where nobody talks to you, nobody trusts you, and everybody is looking at you sideways. I could have done that, sure, but I wouldn't have been happy. Who wants a job where you have no function? I mean, when I was in Wichita I was rarely asked about the players I managed in AA ball. And we're talking about Billy Butler and Alex Gordon – the heart of the team today. Nothing like: How does this guy handle a slump? How is this guy to deal with? Nobody ever asked me those questions. So you feel like you have no function. You go to spring training, you get introduced on the first day and then your function is to grab some balls and throw

Does it get any better than meeting Hank Aaron and having your photo taken with a real legend? I was a coach with the Boston Red Sox and Hank was working for the commissioner's office. A lot of people said my batting stance looked like Hank's. He was the tortoise in the tortoise and the hare story – he was just slow and steady and never hit more than 45 home runs in a single season, but when his career was over, he was the all-time home run king and one of the greatest players ever. I think most people still think of him as baseball's all-time home run king.

batting practice. When the team goes on the road, you stay back and throw more batting practice. I might do a little work with a player, but no one ever asked me for my opinion. So I thought I was wasting my time at spring training. I even talked to Dayton about that. Our most recent conversation was after I resigned. I said, "If you guys want me to go to spring training I'll go. If you don't that's fine too." I'm not one of those guys that needed spring training. Some guys need spring training. I've never been one of those guys.

I didn't want to go through six weeks of just throwing batting practice or just hitting ground balls. And I didn't want to be 65 years old and having rotator surgery. I just felt like a lot of teams would take a guy like me and they would say, "Look, this is your guy. I want you to work with this guy." But I think our coaches felt threatened if I worked with someone, and I didn't want anyone to feel uncomfortable, so I just didn't do it. I'd see things that I felt like I could help the young guys with, but the coaches never asked my opinion. That was the hardest thing in spring training – having the guys you managed, the guys you knew – and not feeling comfortable going up and working with them. I think that was the reason I didn't really like spring training. And it got to the point where I didn't feel comfortable in the broadcast booth, either. I never had a player complain to me, or a member of the player's family. When Rick Ankiel was struggling and all the problems (changing from pitching to becoming a position player), I ran into his wife and she thanked me for all the positive things I said about him. When you played the game, you have a special feeling for the guys who are playing it today. If you didn't play, it would be easy to be critical because you have no idea how hard the game actually is. You know what a guy is going through emotionally, mentally, what he is dealing with. It's tough. You don't need to beat up a guy from the TV booth. That's not right – that's why I could never understand how the team said I was too critical. It was easy for a guy who never played the game to say this guy has a problem but when you've played the game and you've been there and, you know, what a guy is mentally or emotionally going through. And you're not going to add to his list of problems by beating him up on the air. I actually drew energy from the wives, the moms and dads, the fans who came up and complimented me because I wasn't getting anything positive from the team. My approach to the broadcast was simple – I didn't want to be the smartest guy in the booth, but I didn't want to be the dumbest guy in the booth, either. I wanted to keep it simple. Keep it simple, stupid. That was my motto. When I first started preparing for games I would go on the internet and research every player on the opposing team. Ryan would do the same thing and he'd talk about where a guy went to school and his family history and things like that, or where he was drafted. So I let Ryan talk about that stuff and I just talked about the game. I would get my information from the coaches, from the players, and I always tried to talk from a player or coach or manager's perspective. And I think our fans liked that. And on replays, I tried to tell the fans what to look for – I tried to coach them. I was doing my best to teach them something every inning of every game. What I wanted to do in the replay was point out a detail that would make the person at home go, "Wow, okay now I understand," whether it just be coaching points or an attention to detail. I really thought that was what made me popular with the fans because I was teaching them something every game.

"The Red Sox were refreshing because all they talked about was winning."

I left the Royals in 1990 and only went to one game the next year. In 1992 I started working for another organization and I found that baseball could be fun again because you see everybody trying to get to the same place. The Red Sox were refreshing because all they talked about was winning. They didn't talk about playing .500 baseball and they didn't talk about winning 82 games. The fans were there every night and they really got into the games – just like Royals fans used to do when we played back in the '70s and '80s. In 1995 Boston won the division and that was the first time I had been part of a winning team for a long, long time, and it felt so good. If you want to win, you have to put yourself in the right frame of mind and you have to have a front office that gives you every opportunity to win. In Boston, there wasn't any talk of a small market or a big market – it was just win, win, win. And it was fun. The teams that win set high goals so the players have something to strive for. It's tough for a small market team, because you have guys who aren't used to winning and don't know how to win, and you have to set the standards high so they will do everything possible to reach the goals they set. Let the young players develop in the minors, then give them every opportunity to come to the major leagues to succeed. What it all boils down to is this – baseball is a simple game. You either can do the job or you can't do the job and the ones that can do it go on to have great careers and some of the ones who can't do it have great careers as backup guys. Everyone is trying to establish themselves, find a niche. I struggled offensively when I first joined the Royals and I think that made me appreciate all the struggles I see guys go through today. Alex Gordon struggled when he first came up, and now he's a Gold Glove outfielder. Eric Hosmer has struggled and Mike Moustakas has struggled. You can tell that Hosmer and Moustakas are going to be great players and Gordon is on the verge of being a great player – but you need to see them produce three, four, five years in a row before you can really tell what type of players they are going to be.

I was part of a transition where I saw young guys struggle and then go on to become great players. I was actually proud of our team when I came to the big leagues, because when we were expansion team, we never got killed by every team every night. We worked hard. We had some success and we built on that success. We traded for the guys who became the heart of the team – Hal, Big John, Amos, Cookie, Freddie. We played on turf, and the Royals were smart enough to base our team on the turf. We were athletic and fast and played great defense. Those guys had high accountability, and when I came to the big leagues in '73, John Mayberry was my roommate. He told me, "You know, we don't make excuses on this ball club. There is no gray area on this ball club. Either you do the job or you don't do the job. You make mistakes, admit your mistakes and get better from your mistakes. I don't care if it is raining. I don't care if it is sunny. I don't care if the ball took a bad hop. I don't care if it is snowing. I don't care what it is when a writer comes to you and asks you why you didn't make the play say, "I screwed it up.' Nothing more to say, just say, 'I made a mistake and let's move on.'" He said when you do it that way, you are not dwelling on that play when the next hitter comes up, now you are thinking about the next play. So they had a real good way of bringing new guys into the game because they basically took all the excuses away. When George and Duke and Leonard and those guys arrived, everything got better, and by 1976, we won a division championship. We were such a tight-knit team. All we wanted to do was talk baseball and play baseball.

"They broke my heart."

I think when something really matters to you, when you love something, and they take it away, it's tough to come back from. The Royals broke my heart. They made me feel like I never mattered. It's like that door mat that everybody steps on everyday – that was me. I was the doormat. I tried so hard to be an asset and never got there. You try so hard to show up in so many different ways, to show your value, to show your worth, and it doesn't matter. You are willing to suffer through the insults of not being interviewed for jobs, not given courtesy phone calls for jobs, and you also suffer through the fact that you are working with guys who you know could benefit from your point of view. And you question one thing in 15 years - my salary- and look what happened. That's when you know you're fighting a losing battle. And I didn't really like it being reduced to a money situation; I always thought I was more valuable than that. After a while, I went from being a real proud guy to feeling like I was worthless, that what I was doing didn't matter. My health was starting to suffer and I thought, "You know, this is just not worth it." But when I made that decision, I immediately felt better. I didn't want them to control my integrity. You can control your integrity, and that was my only concern coming out of this whole deal. They can have the job, but they can't have my integrity. I have been gracious in so many different ways, but this episode with the Royals really has turned me off on baseball. I've been able to meet so many neat people since the Royals let me go me; people that I probably never would have met had I remained with the Royals, so there have been some positive things to come out of all of this.

16 "The one thing that stood out from the event at the Kauffman Center was that all the guys there were winners."

WHEN I THINK BACK TO THAT EVENT AT THE KAUFFMAN CENTER FOR the Performing Arts, one word comes to mind – winners. Jim Sundberg was the best defensive catcher, Hal McRae was the best designated hitter, Bret Saberhagen was the best pitcher over a five-year period, John Schuerholz was the architect of our world championship team, and even having Reggie Jackson there – one of our biggest rivals, the straw that stirred the drink – it was amazing to share that with the fans who wanted to take part in a celebration of Mr. K's life through some great videos and our conversation from the stage. Those were a group of hard-nosed players who loved the game. Sunny was one of the last guys to catch every game, Hal worked hard to make himself a great hitter, and while Sabes had as much fun as anyone I ever played with, he worked hard, too. It was special to see John Schuerholz, because he was the last successful general manager this team has had. They talk about all his success in Atlanta – and they were the most successful team in the National League in the 1990s, but he started that success in Kansas City and I don't think he gets enough credit. When we needed a piece to the puzzle, he went out and got it. And look at all the great young pitchers we developed in our farm system. You look back at those days and wonder where they went. You knew you were on the verge of something good in 1984 when Jackson, Saberhagen and Gubicza all came up. They didn't just have good arms, they had the desire and the guts to compete. We didn't keep them together for as long as anyone of us would have liked, but money forces issues in baseball that the players and the fans don't like. I know John had to make some tough decisions and I never asked him if the money issues in Kansas City were a reason he went to Atlanta, but it had to be tough to start all over again. But you look at what happened in Atlanta and it proves that with the right people making the right decisions and money for a good payroll, you can have success. A lot of the Royals' problems started in 1994, the year of the strike. After that season – which was really pretty successful with David Cone winning the Cy Young Award and the team having a winning record – management decided to get rid of most of the veterans. They got rid of Cone and Brian McRae and the other veterans on the team. That's when they started to bring up the young guys like Johnny Damon, Mike Sweeney and Michael Tucker. And they put so much pressure on those kids – they were going to be good players, but they came up too soon and the Royals didn't have the pitching, and the team started to lose on a regular basis. I think that was the beginning of an era where the team lost its pride. In 1996 the team finished last for the first time in team history – and we'd been around since 1969. In 2002 we lost 100 games in a single season for the first time. It was a case of one year where you have good hitting, the next year you have good pitching. There was a lot of flip flopping back and forth between hitting, pitching and defense, and they never could get everything going in the same season. They fell below .500 for the first time in team history, and I can't speak for all the guys who played back when I was playing, but that was a real low mark for me. From there, the problems just seemed to snowball out of control. They went from Bob Boone to Tony Muser to Tony Pena to Buddy Bell, and no manager seemed to have any success. But the lowest point of all came to me in 2002 on the last game of the season. I was talking to Teresa and I told her that I was going to look at the lineup that day, and if it looked like they were going to try to win the game, to keep from losing 100 games for the first time in franchise history, I was going to watch the game. If not, I was going to cut the grass. I looked at the lineup and told Teresa that I was going out to cut the grass. I wanted to know if the team had any pride at all – were they going to play their best players or just phone it in? When I saw the lineup and I saw a lot of the top guys weren't playing, I just turned the TV off and went out and cut the grass (Kit Pellow hit fourth that game and Aaron Guiel hit fifth and they were a combined 1-for-7). Then I read comments in the paper the next day where guys were saying, "If you don't finish in first place, who cares?" I think those are the type of comments you make to keep from saying, "we stink." I can't even begin to tell you how bad I felt that whole day. The Royals, one of the proudest franchises in baseball in the 1970s and 80s, was a sub.500 franchise with its first 100-loss season. The big headline on the top of the sports page the next day was a big 100 in the middle of the paper, with 50 L's on one side and 50 L's on the other. If that wasn't embarrassing to the team, I don't know what would be. I was working in the front office at the time and I cut that article out and kept it in my desk the whole year. Where did our pride go that year? I kept hearing people say if you don't finish first, it doesn't matter. Doesn't matter? I'd rather finish third or fourth than last. I'd do anything to avoid losing 100 games – and this franchise has lost 100 games four times. When I hear someone say, "At least we didn't lose 100 games," I can't believe a comment like that, either. If you're last, you're last. If you hit 19 homers, 20 sounds better. If you win 19 games, 20 sounds better. Doesn't a .300 batting average sound better than a .299 average? It was just a philosophical difference I had with a lot of people in the organization. There were a lot of money issues, but money issues have nothing to do with pride.

I don't know the story behind this photo but I don't look very happy, do I?

When I was in the front office, I spent a lot of time in the minor leagues, evaluating players, talking to managers and coaches and things like that. So I didn't really get into the trade side, deciding whether to trade guys or dealing with a guy's salary. I did some minor-league salaries, but none of the big stuff, so the only thing I knew about came from listening to guys talk about trades and talk about salaries and things like that. The biggest thing to me was just how people talked. It was all about money – that's all I heard about. I kept wondering how the organization was going to put a competitive team on the field if it was just all about money. I think everyone was trying their best, but nothing ever panned out. Even 2004, when we signed Benito Santiago and Juan Gonzalez – two big-name free agents and former all-stars – that was a disaster. They got hurt, didn't play and cost the team a lot of money. And when things like that happened, you pushed yourself back a step instead of taking a step forward. And the team took a lot of steps back, and very few steps forward. By 2006, I was managing at AA Wichita and had guys like (future Cy Young Award winner) Zack Greinke and (all-star) Billy Butler and (Gold Glove outfielder) Alex Gordon. Those were the guys the Royals were banking on. Gordon just signed the big contract and I know they like Butler and they traded Greinke for some guys (Lorenzo Cain and Alcides Escobar) who will help the club on an everyday basis. But this team is never going to win like it did in the old days, unless it gets better pitching. I mean, if pitching doesn't perform for you, none of the other stuff is really going to matter. I think the thing that hurt the Royals, and you go back to 1996 when they finished last for the first time in team history, and had the opportunity to draft the best players – they couldn't, because of money issues. They knew that even if they got the best prospect, they would have trouble signing that player, whereas a team like Tampa Bay went out and drafted the best player, signed the best player and look how they have improved from within their own minor league system. Today, it seems like the Royals are always managing their team in a developmental mode, and that's hard on the manager, the fans, everyone. You should always manage to win and I think the accountability should always be high at this level. That's why you're here and that's how you're going to find who can handle it mentally and emotionally. So that's why I say the evaluation process is always going to be the key and the key to success is knowing what to keep and what to throw away. And that's where the Royals are right now.

I thought they did the right thing signing (Gardner-Edgerton High School's) Bubba Starling. He cost the team a lot of money, but he was a hometown kid with all the tools. Every time you draft a kid out of high school, you're taking a gamble. No one thought that (Fort Osage High School graduate Albert) Pujols would become the best player in the game for a while, and he was in the Royals own backyard. It's a gamble, but after they missed out on Pujols, they almost had to sign Startling, and now, it's a waiting game to see if he can produce at the major league level. We've had some really bad No. 1 picks – so have a lot of other teams – but when you're at the bottom of the division every year and have the chance to make a high draft pick, those bad picks become more glaring.

I can even point back to 1985, when we won the World Series. We lost a lot of guys from that team and brought up AAA guys who were good players, but we never took off as a team after 1985 – Dick was diagnosed with cancer, Sabes had some injuries, some free agents didn't pan out – then it all went downhill after the strike in 1994.

It was a money thing. They didn't have a lot of money, and by that time Mr. K was gone and we had a young team that just didn't play well. Hal was the last Royals manager who was fired with a winning record. I remember when I was a young player and Hal was the guy I looked up to, he was the guy who helped all the young guys on the club learn what it was like to be a big leaguer. I read a quote in the paper where someone said Hal was fired because he didn't work well with the young guys on the team. Then Bob Boone came in and it was almost like a comedy of errors after that.

17 "During all this with the Royals, she made sure I was okay."

I DON'T KNOW THAT I WOULD HAVE SURVIVED ALL THIS WITH THE Royals if it hadn't been for Teresa. After I returned from Boston in 1996, I started working for Blue Cross Blue Shield. I was sitting in the lunch room with former Chiefs great Otis Taylor. Teresa came in to post something on a bulletin board. I asked Otis "Who is that?" Otis told me she worked in Human Resources. I told Otis I had to meet her. One day I had an appointment in HR and I went in hoping I would see her, and I did. We began talking.

"I didn't work there very long," Teresa said. "It was supposed to be a temporary job and Frank was just a scary guy to me. I had no idea who he was – just a good looking guy who was scary. He was good looking and seemed like a nice guy, but I was going through a divorce and was separated and mentally, I was like – no way, no!"

I also was separated and about to be divorced, and we just had a general conversation. I asked her what she was doing for Christmas, and she said she was staying home. She was separated and said her boys would be with their dad and that she was staying home, so I asked her why she was staying home and she kind of shrugged – like, "Why are you asking me that?" I said you haven't had the right offer. Then I thought, *she must think this guy is a jerk.*

"Oh, I did – I did think he was a jerk," Teresa said, laughing. "Where does a comment like that come from? I wasn't doing anything for Christmas, but I thought he was a guy using a line."

She brought this ball to my office, and it was all different colors, I took a real baseball out of my desk and signed it. I took her to lunch the day after Christmas, we talked on and off, and it took three months before we considered ourselves dating. We got married October 7 of

2000. She has been great – she's laid back, very thorough, organized, very attentive to any situation going on. She is independent - if I want to go hunting or fishing she says, "See you later." She lets me do what I need to do and she does what she needs to do. She has a big family. During all this with the Royals, she made sure I was okay. She runs interference, she takes care of ticket requests, appearances, things like that. She makes sure I get enough rest. I don't know where I'd be or what I'd be without her.

"When we dated, we'd go to lunch or talk on the phone – no one really knew we were dating," Teresa said. "He did invite me to attend an event after work, and all these people were all over him – and I thought that was nice, but I didn't understand what he meant to the people in Kansas City, his fans. They adored him. I was like, "Okay, wow!" My father was a big fan; I'm sure he would know what a big deal Frank was. But I didn't.

Teresa's dad and Uncle Harry watched games all the time, when they needed a beer, she got him a beer. She was aware of my coaching career, and that gave her some insight. She was there during my coaching career and front office career, She is a proud person and she would give you the shirt off her back, but if she gets crossed, that's it.

"There have been things that have happened, but none as hurtful as this last incident," Teresa said. "And that hurt me – but we got through it."

Teresa gives a lot, and now we're figuring out what direction we're going to go. When we first started dating I told her that dating me might be the hardest thing she'd ever done in her life, and after the past few years, I'd bet she agrees with that.

Teresa, along with my family – my brother and sisters, my children, Frank, Terrance, Courtney, Adrianne, Teresa's children, Michael, Joseph, Daryl and Jordan – are so important to me. They're the reason I can get out of bed every day – especially the really bad days – and know that everything is going to be all right. When you think about your family, it's how funny the little things pop into your head. Back in 1985, Courtney was in kindergarten and I took her to school one morning after we won the World Series. All the kids were excited, and most mornings the moms took the kids to school. But

I took her that morning and was walking her to class and the kids started saying, "Frank White! Frank White!" All this World Series stuff was up on the wall and on the bulletin boards and while all this is going on, Courtney looks up at me and says, "I know who you are." And I look at her and ask her who. "You're Frank White." I just bent over laughing. To her, for so many years, I was daddy, but today, I'm Frank White. I think it was the first time it registered with her that her daddy wasn't just her daddy, that other people knew who her daddy

Here I am playing Mr. Mom before one of the Royals Father-Son games in the 1970s. Whats do you think of Terrance's custom-fit uniform? I think he's a lot more interested in his bottle than he is playing baseball with his dad. It's a lot of fun for me to see a photo from that wonderful period in my life.

was. And I thought, *Whoa, this is going to be an interesting morning.* And it was – and it's been interesting every day since.

"It has been interesting," said Frank White III, Frank's oldest son, who is the director of recruiting for Heartland Financial Group. "Growing up as Frank White III was almost surreal. I was born before my dad even went to the academy, so I always knew him as a ball player. We'd go to the stadium with my friends to watch the Royals and I'd see my dad, George, Hal and the rest of the players and my friends saw them as George Brett and Hal McRae and Frank White the Royals players and I just saw them as my dad and George and Hal. It was so cool for them, but it was just another day at the park for me, visiting my dad and watching a game.

"I know one thing about growing up as Frank White – I made sure I never got in trouble. If my name had been Joe White, it might not have been as important to me, but I never wanted to do anything to embarrass my dad or my family. My name kept me from doing a lot of dumb things and I am grateful for that. I never went into a restaurant and said, "My name is Frank White," expecting to get a free cheeseburger. Because my dad played pro ball, we got to do some amazing things as a family and I will always remember the trips to spring training, the World Series – there were some great times."

Younger sister Adrianne Russell, the coordinator of public programs and special events for the Beach Museum of Art at Kansas State University, agrees.

"I was in the fifth grade when the Royals won the World Series and it was a big deal to be Frank White's daughter," Adrianne said, chuckling. "When I was little, I never understood why everyone wanted to stop my dad and talk to him, get a photo or get an autograph. But as I got older, I began to understand. When I was young, I thought it was that way with everyone's dad. But, as I got older, I realized I had a pretty special dad who meant a lot to the people in Kansas City. He is a real Kansas City icon, a man who has left an amazing mark on this city – which is also his hometown. I am so proud of him and so proud to be his daughter."

Courtney Prugh, a kindergarten-through-eighth-grade art teacher in Fort Worth, Texas, echoes her sister's comments.

"I don't remember him taking me to school and me telling him, "I know who you are. You are Frank White," because I was in kindergarten. But I do remember all the celebration following the World Series and I remember how special it was when daddy took me to school. People would ask for his autograph, and if he couldn't sign it at that moment he would get their address and send them an autograph in the mail. He loved his fans and they loved him. Some of my best memories are centered around my birthday, which was when our family would go to spring training in Florida. I always got to celebrate my birthday in Florida – we'd go to Sea World, see all the sights and I got to spend it with my family, especially my dad, who was gone so much of the time because of playing baseball. We spent as much time with him as we could, especially down in spring training."

Terrance White, a stay-at-home-dad who is about to return to school, lives just outside of Vancouver, Canada, also has vivid memories of his father as a Royals player.

"It was always so much fun to go watch him at the park or watch the Royals on TV because our dad was out there playing – and let's face it, that was cool," Terrance said. "When you are the son of a major league player, you see things a bit differently. I always thought of my dad's job as his job – it was no different than my friends' dads' jobs – until I got older and realized it was pretty special. No one was asking their dads for their autographs. And they didn't get to go to the World Series or spring training. All the kids always looked forward to Opening Day, because we didn't have to go to school. We went to the stadium. My mom and dad made sure we had a normal family life, and we did – we had a great time together. It was special being Frank White's son, but even more special being part of a great family."

18

"At times like that, I get humble. It's almost like you want to just put your head down, because it's so unexpected."

I KNEW THE ALL-STAR GAME WAS COMING TO TOWN, AND I KNEW that I wasn't going to take part in any of the festivities at the stadium. But I wanted to take part in the festivities in and around Kansas City. The mayor, The Negro Leagues Baseball Museum and other places made sure that I had the chance to be a part of the things I enjoyed the most – the festivities where I could be with the fans and with my friends – the guys I played with. It all started out with a few radio interviews. There was a Gold Glove event at the Negro League Baseball Museum where Ozzie Smith and I announced the all-time greatest fielders in the history of the Negro Leagues. Each one of them received a Gold Glove, and an honorary glove was given to Buck O'Neil.

An event took place at the Negro Leagues Museum, located at 18th and Vine in downtown Kansas City, Misssouri.

Hall of Famer Ozzie Smith, a 13-time Gold Glove winner, and Frank White, the Kansas City Royals Hall of Fame second baseman who won eight Gold Gloves, were on hand to greet a group of fans who received a commemorative Negro Leagues Gold Glove baseball, as the winners of the first Negro Leagues Gold Glove team were announced by perennial all-star infielders who earned the nicknames "The Wizard of Oz," and "Smooth."

"Today is a history-making event," Negro Leagues spokesman Bob Kendrick told a standing-room-only crowd at the museum's Field of Legends display. "We took a great deal of time and dedication to select the Negro Leagues Gold Glove team – a team with just nine players. We

could have had nine teams with nine players and still not recognized all the deserving nominees. And we have two legendary Gold Glove winners to make the announcement. Does it get any better than being here with Ozzie Smith and Kansas City's own Frank White?"

A panel that included Negro Leagues historians and former Negro Leagues star and Hall of Famer Monte Irvin selected the elite group that was announced by White and Smith. White, who earned the nickname "Smooth," from former teammate Darrell Porter, drew a two-minute ovation that shook the walls of the museum, and Smith – known as "The Wizard of Oz," to a generation of baseball fans, followed with his own rousing ovation. Also on hand was Mike Thompson, the senior vice president of marketing for Rawlings, the sporting goods company that has produced the iconic trophies that signify fielding excellence since 1957.

"This is Rawlings' 125th anniversary," Thompson said, "and we have established a timeline of great moments in Rawlings history. This event will become a part of that timeline. Having Frank and Ozzie take part makes it even more special."

The Gold Glove winners were Walter "Buck" Leonard, first base; Newt Allen, second base; Willie Wells, shortstop; Ray Dandridge, third base; James "Cool Papa" Bell, Martin Dihigo and Oscar Charleston, outfield; Raleigh "Biz" Mackey, catcher; and Leon Day, pitcher. Buck O'Neil, the longtime Kansas City resident and baseball ambassador who has a statue outside the Major League Baseball Hall of Fame in Cooperstown, N.Y., was also recognized with an honorary Gold Glove.

"It took me about 15 seconds to say I would love to be a part of this when I got the call from Bob (Kendrick)," said Smith, long considered the greatest defensive shortstop in the history of the major leagues. "When I heard about the Gold Gloves for the Negro Leagues players and learned that Frank was going to be a part of this, I couldn't wait to say yes." Frank, who grew up in downtown Kansas City and lived just three blocks from Negro Leagues and Hall of Fame pitching legend Satchel Paige, said the ceremony and the museum both hold a special place in his heart.

"I was on one of the first committees that talked about having a museum to honor the players from the Negro League," said the premier second baseman of his era. "At first, they didn't have any money, so the members of the committee paid the rent on a revolving basis.

"Now, we have this museum. I used to watch the Negro League games at Municipal Stadium (which was located at 22nd and Brooklyn in Kansas City, Mo.) and remember a first baseman named 'Nature Boy' Kirby. He played first base in a straw skirt and would sit down on a stool during the game. Some of the teams would hold infield practice without a ball – they'd go through all the routines, turning double plays and fielding ground balls – but it was minus the ball. They were showmen, but they were also great athletes."

Smith said an elderly Negro Leagues player paid him the ultimate compliment. "The greatest compliment anyone ever bestowed on me," Smith said, "came from a former Negro Leagues player who told me, 'You could have played with us.'"

While the Negro League players received their Gold Gloves, I received something even more special. When I was announced, I received a standing ovation that a friend of mine said lasted about two minutes. I just walked out to the stage and everyone started to clap and cheer. At times like that, I get humble. It's almost like you want to just put your head down, because it's so unexpected. I remember Ozzie got a nice ovation, too. I was glad, because I was almost

This is the award I received from the Negro Leagues Baseball Museum when I was honored with the Jackie Robinson Legacy Award for Lifetime Achievement. I've received a few trophies over the years, but this one is one of the most special. I keep it upstairs where I know right where it is.

embarrassed by the ovation I received. But like I've said so many times, that's the fans in Kansas City. I love them, and I guess they still love me. I remember back in January, when I was asked to do a fashion show. It was for a local charity and Teresa and I were going to be the last two models to walk the runway. Out of the blue, the whole place stood up and gave us a standing ovation. I looked at Teresa and she just started to cry. I was kind of stuck, everyone is clapping, she's crying and I don't think we even modeled our clothes. I'm like, "Oh, my gosh, I have to get her off the stage," but we couldn't leave because the people kept clapping and cheering. I wanted her to get off stage so she could kind of compose herself, but we couldn't leave. The applause was almost deafening.

It was almost like that at the Negro Leagues Baseball Museum. Willie Wilson was there. We were talking and he's like, "Man, this town loves you." I just hope Ozzie didn't feel bad. If it had been in St. Louis, I'm sure he would have received the bigger ovation. Maybe I'm a little bit naïve, but when stuff like that happens, it still catches me off guard. I never expect it, and never will. I just don't see myself in that light. I don't see myself as a celebrity, I just see myself as someone who loves this community and enjoys being with the people.

I think that's one reason I enjoyed Fan Fest so much. It was at Bartle Hall and it covered the entire second floor. Mike Schmidt and Cal Ripken were doing interviews and conducting clinics, Rollie Fingers and Gaylord Perry were signing autographs, and there were all sorts of vendors and memorabilia dealers. I'd never seen anything like it. I did a two-hour autograph session for Hot 103 – a local radio station – and I really didn't think there would be many fans there. If anyone in Kansas City wants my autograph, they probably have it five or six times. But I arrived at the autograph table and the line wound all through the signing area – it was full. There had to have been 2,000 people in that line. I just thought to myself, "Oh my goodness." Again, I was overwhelmed. I stayed over my signing time because if someone waited that long to get an autograph, I wanted to make sure they got an autograph and got to shake my hand and talk for a second or two. All the people had such nice things to say. They had their

their quick little stories, but most of all it was, "We miss you" or "We miss you on TV" or "We miss you not being with the Royals" and that type of thing. They were all so nice – they really made me feel good and I was supposed to be there to make them feel good. As I signed, I kept looking at the line, and it never seemed to get any shorter. But we finally got through it and they all waved or applauded when I left. I wanted to thank them, and they were thanking me. I never did get to walk through all the Fan Fest booths and see the displays or talk to any of the other players who were down there. You just couldn't, because of security reasons. When I left the autograph signing – and I'd been there 2 ½ to three hours – there were still people chasing me down trying to get things signed. Those were the people I had to disappoint because they wouldn't let me stop for something like that because it would have created a real problem for the fans trying to walk around

I have some amazing fans. Someone put this montage together that featured some of my career highlights. I think the reason my fans are so loyal is because I treat them the same way I would want to be treated – with respect. Sharing my career with my family and our great fans has been one of the highlights of my career with the Royals.

and see everything. The Fan Fest people told me I could come back and see it all before they let the fans in, but I was so busy I never got the chance to do that.

Of all the things associated with the All-Star Game, my favorite event took place at the Kauffman Center, where members of the 1985 Royals – general manager John Schuerholz, catcher Jim Sundberg, designated hitter Hal McRae, World Series MVP and Cy Young Award winner Bret Saberhagen and I were able to talk about the World Series and honor Mr. K. Reggie Jackson was even there, talking about all the great rivalry games against the Royals, and I was impressed with how much he knew about our team and how much he remembered about the World Series – even sitting in Dick's office with me in the ninth inning of Game 6 during our comeback victory. You see, it was important for me to share those memories – especially my memories of Mr. K – with the people I shared that World Series victory with. The celebration for Mr. K was the same night as the Celebrity Softball Game at Kauffman Stadium, but the Kauffman Center was still packed. Mr. K's daughter, Julia Irene, was there and it was one of those nights that you never forget. It was perfect. They did a nice videotape montage of Mr. K and how he brought the Royals to Kansas City after Charlie Finley moved the A's to Oakland. There were a lot of older fans – fans my age – who were in attendance and you could see a few tears out in the audience. I love the Royals, and I will always love the Royals – the Royals from my generation. The Royals who worked together, played together and won together. And I would have never been a part of that if it hadn't been for Mr. K. Sharing the stage and the memories with my former teammates and John Schuerholz brought back the greatest memories – it's funny, every time you're around those people, you recall things that you'd forgotten about. But none of us will ever forget 1985 or Mr. K.

Because of my situation with the team, I didn't expect to take part in any all-star ceremony at the game, but I thought it would have been great if the Royals would have somehow honored Amos and Big John. They were in the All-Star Game in Kansas City in 1973 and they each played and got a hit – Amos got a couple of hits in that game.

That's why I was so proud of Teresa for getting together with Chris Browne and honoring Amos, Big John, Freddie, Hal, Mickey Cobb – the Royals all-stars from the past – at a T-Bones game. The fans loved seeing those guys and those guys had so much fun talking. There was a lot of talking going on at that game. It really made me proud that Mayor James wanted me to represent the city in all the festivities away from the game but I wish Amos and Big John could have somehow been all-star ambassadors. Once again, we have to remember our heritage and there you have two players who played for the Royals in the first All-Star Game at Royals Stadium, and the only team that really honored them in a special way was the T-Bones. Amos and John have such great memories from that game. Amos idolized Hank Aaron and there they were, on the same field. Same thing for Big John – he was a big fan of Hank Aaron's, too. But who wasn't a fan of Hank Aaron? He was such a great player – and you look back at Willie Mays and Hank Aaron and all those great all stars who went on to become Hall of Famers. That was a pretty special night in Kansas City baseball history, and I wish our two former all stars would have been more a part of this year's game. They weren't honored in front of 42,000 fans at Kauffman Stadium, but they got a standing ovation from the 7,000 or 8,000 fans who were at the T-Bones game that night.

That was a night that brought back a lot of memories, just like the celebration of Mr. K at the Kauffman Center for the Performing Arts. The Kauffman Center is just amazing, and I know Mr. K would have been proud of Julia Irene and everyone else who worked so hard to make that event so special. After that, things got a little hectic – like the day of the All-Star Game where Teresa and I went with Jackson County Sheriff Mike Sharp, in his patrol car, to visit four all-star sites, just before and during the game. Sheriff Sharp, who is a good friend and a great guy, was in full uniform and he had the lights on and Teresa and I were in the back seat and she's pleading, "Go faster, go faster! Turn on your lights!" It was so much fun – the looks we got from the people on the side of the street were great. They had to be wondering what was going on – where are those people going?

"I wasn't around in 1985, but I have seen the highlights and know what you meant to your team when the Royals won the World Series. But I know – and admire you – for what you did during the All-Star Game festivities in and around Kansas City. What you did in 1985 did not go unnoticed, and what you did in representing the city at the All-Star Game festivities did not go unnoticed. You were an ambassador for an entire city, and we thank you"

Jermaine Reed
Kansas City Councilman

The first stop was the Kansas City Zoo. People were still setting up when we got there. They had a big tent and concessions – they were selling ballpark food – and all these chairs were lined up. You could tell they were ready for a party. And they had this huge TV. The zoo is right next to Starlight Theater and it kind of reminded me of what it might be like to watch a ballgame at Starlight. They had the chairs, the big TV and you were under the lights. I said a few words on behalf of the mayor, I don't even really remember what I said, and the fans seemed to appreciate that fact that we came by. I was so impressed by Mayor Sly James, who said that you didn't have to be at the game to get the all-star experience. And we were proving that. Wherever we went, people seemed to be having a great time. After I spoke, I signed some autographs, posed for some pictures and then it was off to 18th and Vine, down by the Negro Leagues Baseball Museum. We jumped on 71 Highway and got there fast – it was like being in a movie, Sheriff Sharp can drive that patrol car – and he got us wherever we needed to be fast. When we got to 18th and Vine, there were already 300 people there. I just quit being surprised by what I saw, because nothing Kansas City does surprises me anymore. Out the back door of the museum is a courtyard and people were lined up everywhere. They brought their lawn chairs and they had a band playing and I basically did the same thing I did at zoo – I talked a few minutes, thanked them for participating and then it was off to Guadalupe Center. Mike introduced me down there and that was really special. The Guadalupe Center is in the historic Hispanic part of downtown Kansas City and there were a lot of people there, too. I think baseball is universal, and this whirlwind night certainly proved that was true. There weren't as many people at Guadalupe Center, because many of the people who visit the center are elderly, and they were home watching the game so they didn't have to be out in the hot sun. I was really impressed with the Guadalupe Center, and they made all of us feel right at home.

"Frank White is Kansas City. This is his town."
Kansas City Mayor Sly James

Again, a speech, a few autographs and then it was off to our final destination – Crown Center in downtown Kansas City. They had hot dogs and were set up on the east side of Crown Center by the fountains. They also had the giant TV and a lot of people there in lawn chairs, and they seemed to enjoy themselves. And being at Crown Center brought back some great memories for me. We had our parades following the 1980 and 1985 World Series down by Crown Center.

I love to teach and I love to talk baseball. Here I am in the T-Bones clubhouse visiting with former Blue Springs High School all-state catcher Bubby Williams, who was with the T-Bones earlier this season. His love of the game makes him a special young man and I hope one day he can say he played in the big leagues.

Like we have talked about before, the first parade caught me off guard because we lost the World Series to the Phillies. I always wondered what this town would do to celebrate if we won, and I found out in 1985. The parade was so crazy. Fans were throwing confetti from office buildings, and from the side of the street, and it was getting under the old cars we were riding in and it was causing some real problems. I think that the car Sabes was in caught fire. And I think there were some problems with Dick's car, too. You drive by Crown Center and you see the Liberty Memorial, and that's where we talked to the fans – and there were thousands of them there on the Liberty Memorial lawn. And that's when you start to get nostalgic – not just about the 1980 and 1985 teams, but the teams before those championship teams that paved the way to those teams and those years.

"Can you imagine someone throwing 12 innings today?"

When I played for the Royals, there were some bad times – every player experiences some bad times – but there were so many good times, and the good times always outweigh the bad. Even with what I'm going through today, it's the good times I will always remember. I just wish today's fans could have seen the real Royals play – George, Willie, Cowens – the guys who came up through the system – Amos, Big John, Hal – the guys who came over in trades. When we needed to make a trade, we always made the right trade, just like getting Willie Aikens from the Angels in 1980. We always made the right trade. We get Freddie, Freddie goes and U.L. steps in – Amos goes and Willie moves over from left field to center. And the pitching – that was the key. It was unbelievable. And we didn't have the big 20-game Cy Young winners until Sabes came along in the mid 1980s, but we had the guys who knew how to win, like Busby. I remember one game in California, I think it might have been 1973 and he pitches 12 innings. He wouldn't come out of that game – he was such a gamer, such a big game guy. I was never around guys like that until I got to the big leagues. Jack McKeon was managing back then and every team had a guy like Buzz who would take the ball and go out and give you nine innings – or 12 innings – whatever it took to win. But you know, his arm was never the same. I don't know if that night had anything to do with his arm problems, I just know the man is in the Hall of Fame if he would have stayed injury free. Can you imagine someone throwing 12 innings today? Throwing 120 or 130 pitches? It would never happen. The agents would never let it happen; the front office would never let it happen. Today, it's all geared around money, and everyone has too much invested in a pitcher to even let him go nine innings, unless you have a really great pitcher like a (Detroit Cy Young Award winner) Justin Verlander. There are spots to fill in the rotation and they find guys to fill those spots. Today, everyone makes such a big deal about closers. If you can throw strikes, if you can throw first-pitch strikes, you had a decent fastball, decent slider, you can succeed as a closer. If you always come into a game with no one on base, and you get 45 to 50 opportunities a year to pitch, you will do well. I think that's the part of the game that has changed the most. Dick and Quiz were a part of that transformation. Dick didn't want Quiz to pitch with men on base because he wasn't a strikeout closer like Gossage. Quiz didn't throw hard, but he was successful if placed in the right situation, and Dick made sure he was usually in the right situation. There were games where he'd pitch more than one inning, but normally he came in in the ninth and slammed the door shut in our opponent's face.

And I think that's where the game changed, where it became a money making proposition and I think that if you're a closer, then you've gotta come in with a man on base, you gotta be able to shut it down. Look at (former Royals closer) Jeff Montgomery. He wasn't all that overpowering, but he had a good slider and good command, and he got 300 saves. He got the job done for a lot of years with men on base, but once again, in the new era of closers and setup men, you want your closer to only throw the ninth inning. Managers today look at a quality start as six-plus innings. Then you bring in your setup men to get you to the ninth when you bring in your closer. You pay your closer a lot of money, so you use him – even if the setup guys are getting the job done. I don't agree with that, but I'm not making that call.

19 "George had the opportunity to fight for himself and he went out on his own terms. Good for him, he deserved it."

Looking back on all this – it seems like it happened such a long time ago some days, and other days it seems like it happened yesterday – it's about respect. I didn't get any respect from the Royals. When someone busts their butt and does everything that is asked of them, they should be respected. You should not use that as a means to take something away from that person. You should pat them on the back and thank them for what they did. At least, that's how I feel. I never had a bad letter written about me, no bad phone calls, I have been gracious in so many ways to our fans, our sponsors, Royals employees – it just comes back to respect.

I had respect for the Royals. I had respect for the people I worked with, and there are people in the organization who I will always respect. But I am done letting people run me down, talk about me, not treat me with the respect I deserve. The harder I worked, the worse I was treated. Sometimes you get rewarded for hard work, and I wasn't getting rewarded. I'm a big boy – I don't need a pat on the back every day. But I felt like I was getting punished. Despite what happened, there are some positives. I have met so many unique people outside of baseball who I would have never had the chance to meet if I had been in the broadcasting booth. The whole landscape of Major League Baseball is changing. You look around front offices today and you don't see many baseball people. You don't see many strong, former baseball players on staffs. You don't see that, except for maybe Arizona. You create paranoia with staffs like that…and that was certainly the case in Kansas City.

The atmosphere in baseball – at least in Kansas City – is dysfunctional. Just about every player who left this team left on bad terms, except George. George had the opportunity to fight for himself, and he went out on his own terms. Good for him, he deserved it. It was like they were trying to embarrass him when he was part of that group that tried to buy the team before the Glass family bought it. That wasn't right. I thought it was great that he had the tour around the league, the standing ovations, the honors – a Hall of Fame player like George should go out like that. I was not looking for that, but he showed everyone how it should be done. Hal, Amos, Willie, myself, we didn't want to come back when we left. I think it should have been better. It was more like a corporate world where you get your pink slip, they walk you to the door and show you the way out. They pushed me away from the guys. You don't win championships by being non-communicative. That's a scenario that needs to improve on this club. People would say a lot of things about people – a lot of it was said behind their back – but in the end, people just want to be respected. As long as you respect people, things work out. You can hammer stuff out, get stuff worked out, get up from the table, shake hands and it's all cool. But when you don't have respect, nothing is going to happen. A lot of people can't take a deep breath and say that makes sense. Some people don't like being around someone who is a little more intelligent than they are. They don't like to compromise, because they see compromise as losing.

"They broke my heart, but they weren't going to break my pride."

My friends, my family, my love of Kansas City – those are the things that kept me here after I was fired. I was torn apart, I was disappointed, mad and upset. They broke my heart, but they weren't going to break my pride. I was ready to pack my bags and move to Arizona, where I had a home my son was renting. I just wanted to get out of town. But Chris Browne kept me here.

Chris is the vice president and general manager of the T-Bones, the Independent Baseball League team in Wyandotte County. It's interesting, because Chris was a clubhouse attendant back when we won the World Series. He'd been after me to join the T-Bones since I quit managing in Wichita, but the timing was never right. I heard from Chris about a month after all that stuff happened. He was great – he waited until everything cooled down and when he called, I was happy to talk with him.

"Frank was the perfect fit for our team," Browne said. "I'd wanted him to be on the staff for three or four years. We'd talked about managing, coaching, just about everything. Frank didn't want to manage because of all the responsibilities that go along with that. But he wanted to be around baseball, and we wanted him to be around the young guys on the team."

One of the young guys was former all-state catcher and Blue Springs High School state champion Bubby Williams, who had just been released by the Houston Astros organization.

This is a great photo that was taken this year at a T-Bones game. That's Blue Moon Odom, who was one of the top pitchers for the Kansas City and Oakland A's. The T-Bones honored former A's players and Blue Moon threw out the first pitch. He looks like he could still throw an inning or two.

"I live in Blue Springs, and Frank lives in Lee's Summit," said Williams, who is no longer a part of the T-Bones, "so we'd drive to the park together. Me and Frank White driving to the park together – do you believe that? Frank is such a pro, such a great coach. He's forgotten more about baseball than most of us will ever know, and he loves to teach. It can be 103 degrees out there and Frank's working the guys on hitting, fielding – he's always smiling and loving what he's doing."

That enthusiasm is a character trait manager Kenny Hook appreciates.

"I coach third base, and Frank coaches first," Hook said, "and I look over there and I have to pinch myself to think that Frank White is my first base coach. I tell him what to do – me, telling Frank White what to do. I feel funny doing it. But the first day he told me, 'Kenny, I'm here for you and the team. Whatever you need, just let me know.' I feel like I should be asking him to sign an autograph instead of asking him to go work with a kid in the batting cage. But the kids see how enthusiastic he is, and it wears off on them. They are as amazed by him as I am. He has made us a better club, a much better club."

And that puts a smile on Browne's face.

"We're a better club, and we have a lot more fans this season," Browne said. "Everyone wants to come out and see Frank. And he's loving it. We had a talk the other day and he told me how much he has enjoyed this. I know it's a long drive for him, coming over from Lee's Summit, but he never complains. If we're doing some stuff early, he's here early. If a game runs late, he's here late. He is the ultimate professional."

I look over at Chris and think back when he was a clubbie and I'm so proud of all the good things those kids have done. They are police officers, one works for the mayor (Sly James), one has worked with several of the professional sports teams in town – it was a different time back then. The clubbies were as much a part of the team as the players and coaches and manager. We did things so they could make some extra money – like washing your car or running over to Gates to get some barbeque, because we didn't have the great food in the clubhouse back then that they have today. We looked out for them, and they looked out for us. They'd make some road trips and they kept everything confidential. Nothing got out on the street. And now, Chris is the one person responsible for keeping me in Kansas City.

I lost a lot of money when I was fired. I had to take a hard look at our finances and knew we had to make some adjustments. At the time, moving away from Kansas City seemed like the logical thing. Then, I talked with Chris and coaching suddenly seemed like the logical thing to do. He gave me the option to coach, just home games, and make trips to Wichita, Lincoln, Nebraska, and one to Sioux City, Iowa because the guys want to see me on the bus one time. Chris didn't offer me a job. He offered me a lifeline. At that point, I was pretty low – no, I was *real* low. I was in that area where I wasn't totally depressed, but it was like *how much do I have to do to make them feel I am a trustworthy guy*. I am not out to burn the organization, but I felt like

I don't even know where to begin with George Toma. He's a Hall of Fame groundskeeper who used to let us sneak in and watch A's games when the team played at Municipal Stadium at 22nd and Brooklyn. He would hire kids from the inner city to be on the grounds crew and he treated everyone with so much respect. Even though we had turf, he did little things to make it easier for the guys on the infield. He'd make sure the dirt came right up to the edge of the turf so you didn't get any bad bounces. He's the hardest working guy you could ever be around, and he was honored this year by the T-Bones.

they were not only taking my job, but my reputation – and I spent my whole life building it. The call from Chris gave me an opportunity to stay in baseball, to talk baseball, to teach baseball, which I love. It gave me an opportunity to be visible, to be in front of the people. It was good timing, not just for me, but for Teresa, because she was caught in the middle of all of this. She understood how I felt. She was there supporting me and she understood what was going on. I think it helped her, too, because she worked with Chris and the T-Bones to put together some programs, work with charities, things like that.

"Out of sight, out of mind."

I just laugh when people ask me if I took the T-Bones job because of money. No way! I make a little money, have a few perks, but it's not about the money. It was never about the money. It was more a way of staying visible. You know what they say, "Out of sight, out of mind." I wanted to be visible. After I thought about everything, I'm glad that I didn't let the Royals run me out of town. I was meant to coach. As the analyst for the Royals broadcasts, I was coaching the people watching the game. I'm as coachable as anybody. When I went in the booth, I told Ryan that I was the rookie, he's been doing it 15 years and I would follow his lead. I respect everyone's turf and protocol, on the field, in the front office and in the broadcasting booth. Now, I carry that same philosophy on the field with the T-Bones… and I think it helps the guys to be with someone like me, to be in the trenches with me, ask questions, and help them be more professional – you know, how to act in certain situations. A lot of them missed that, you want them to be as professional on this level as if they were in the big leagues.

It's been a lot of fun getting to be around the people on the Kansas side. They didn't get to see me a lot while I was playing or broadcasting, and now they can see me all the time. The crowds here are more diverse, I see more minorities in the good seats, and from a family perspective, that's just good for baseball.

I enjoy working with Bill Sobbe, who was our bullpen catcher and our manager Kenny Hooks, who is a great guy and I really enjoy being around the young guys.

"Frank is just the best," said Sobbe, a longtime area high school baseball and football coach and administrator. "I'd pay them just to let me sit in the locker room and listen to his stories. It reminds me of the old days at Royals Stadium. Those were some great days – it's a shame the younger fans don't know what it's like to go out to The K and watch guys like Frank and George and Willie and Hal – the guys who were the heart and soul of the team. Now, we have a guy like Frank, who was the best of his generation, working with our young guys and it makes an impact. It really does. Heck, I'm an old dog and it makes an impact on me."

When I joined the T-Bones staff, I didn't really know what to expect. But I knew it was going to be something special when they had their media day. I was in the locker room and some of the guys were

A new uniform, a new team, but the same old smile. I was the first base coach for the Kansas City T-Bones, and I always had plenty to smile about if I was out on the baseball field.

going out to be interviewed. They came back inside and talked about all the television cameras that were there. I popped my head outside the locker room and asked, jokingly, "Is the president here?" I go out of the locker room, and it is wall-to-wall television cameras. I didn't see that many television cameras when I was playing, unless it was a big game against the Yankees or a World Series or playoff game. Everyone was there, and there were a lot of print media, too.

"We'd never had anything like it," Browne said, grinning at the memory. "In years past, we might have the local paper or a television crew or two, but Frank was right, this looked like a presidential news conference." On media day, I thought I would see one or two guys I knew. But goodness, I was shocked. I think that was one of the first times I knew that people weren't pissed at me. The media guys were great, I always did my best to be good to them and they were doing their best to be good to me. I knew the fans weren't upset with me, it was more like everyone understood my situation and now they wanted to give me the chance to let everyone know what I was doing. I don't know how many people would have had the courage to do what I did. You take your whole future and you walk away from it. A lot of people have been there, a lot of people knew how I felt, and they haven't been able to pull the trigger. But my wife told me, "If you want to feel good about yourself, you have to do what you think is right." I had to start thinking about my physical health and my mental health. I couldn't go to work in an atmosphere where people weren't supporting me. They were talking about me, watching me out of the corner of their eye, they didn't trust me – and I didn't know why. But I know one thing: I could not live like that.

My blood pressure went up – the bottom number was 97. And that's way too high. When I made that decision to leave, it went down to the 80s, I felt like the whole world was lifted off my shoulders. I think it's important that people know that initially, I never said I was fired or that they ran me out of the organization. I said it was my decision. I said they made a business decision and I made a personal one – one that saved my life. Sometimes you have to do that in life. My life changed forever, but at all costs you have to maintain your integrity and reputation.

They can take your job away – but I don't think it's right to take your job because some guy is irritated about a decision I made about my community relations job. The amount of money was a concern to the Royals. I even offered to to work as an independent contractor since there were some pension issues.

My mind kept focusing on the manager interviews I sat in on, and phone calls I didn't get, *I just can't do this anymore.* I didn't like myself anymore. I do like myself now. I look back to guys I played with, the guys who got it done. Look at the pride factor of John, George, Hal – we had a pride factor. In the end, you want to be respected for who you are and what you've done. It was an easy decision to make, based on how I felt. Teresa is still torn. Like most mothers, like most wives, she just wants things to be okay. And I told her it's better to be this way than to be mad every day. She knew I was unhappy, she knew I didn't like myself and it had basically been going on every day. So I said, "Let's try it this way."

"He made the right decision," Teresa said. "I've never seen him this happy."

"I'll try stuff I haven't tried before."

I'm a guy who has to stay busy. I have never been a guy who says I absolutely cannot do this or that, in terms of work. I'll try stuff I haven't tried before. That's why I have a job as a sales rep for Precision Roofing. You are dealing with people, dealing with people with integrity – the way all people should be treated. I have been at Broome Cadillac the past three years and they have been great to work with. These are companies, people you trust, and who trust you. It's the same thing with the T-Bones. The Royals should learn from that: You don't just throw people away without really getting to know them, especially when their track record says everything has been good. Anytime ego gets involved in making a business decision, you make the wrong one. I think that's what happened with the Royals. It all comes down to trust. Small thinkers make big messes. I was involved in a big mess, and as much as I loved what I was doing, I had to make a personal decision – and I am so happy I made it.

My stepson Jordan Hurtt, the T-Bones mascot Sizzle and Teresa join me on the field before a special all-star game ceremony in Kansas City, Kan. The T-Bones did a great job recognizing former Kansas City Royals all-stars and Teresa had a role in putting the event together.

18

"I don't know if I'll ever see that statue again."

Every day I get asked the same question. Will I ever go back to Kauffman Stadium? You know that statue of me they have in center field? I don't know if I'll ever see that statue again. I went to Arizona to Fantasy Camp in January and they already had my name off my parking spot. I didn't want them to try and poison the mind of the campers with what they were saying about me, but needless to say, it was my last Fantasy Camp. I have resigned from the board of the Alumni Association – I've done other things I never thought I would consider. But at this time, I feel it is the right thing to do. They say time can heal all wounds…it could happen. It all depends on if I am ever part of a level playing field. If one side or the other wants the upper hand, it's not going to work. Both sides should be concerned about the benefit of the Royals organization. I think the Royals underestimate how the guys I played with feel about the direction of the team. We don't want the team to lose, even though it keeps – the guys from the glory years – our names out there. Fans today wonder why these guys can't win. Why doesn't the team reach out to some of our better players from the past to help the younger guys? A lot of teams reach out to their former players. The Royals ask us to sign autographs or go to spring training and hang out for a week, but not to get down and work with guys? That doesn't happen. That's the wrong way to handle your former players. All the fans have to hold onto are the alumni guys…People say they hold on because that's the last championship. They hold onto it because we were accessible, we were like them. We walked out the front door. We had cars in the parking lot, no special place to park, we signed autographs, told 'em, "See you tomorrow." Our guys were reliable, the fans knew we were going to be there, the lineup would be the same, if they drove 150 miles they knew who was going to play. We left the stadium with our wives and kids, no entourage, no limo dropping you off behind the scoreboard in center field – we were there for them and they appreciated that. They identified with us. The younger generation – kids 9, 10, 11 years old – know who we are.

Across the community, down at the Negro Leagues Museum, T-Bone games, Fan Fest, they know who we are. They know what we stand for because they have heard about it from their families. It's sad that they have never been able to experience it.

> "I go into the inner city, I go places by myself. It's not like the Beatles walking down the street with mobs of people chasing you."

You're never too old to learn something, and goodness, have I ever learned a life's worth of lessons this year. You might not be able to teach an old dog new tricks, but I learned one thing out of this mess – I'm not going to let people take me for granted. All the work I did – on and off the field – when it came to the forefront, it didn't matter. But I know I made a difference in people's lives, and that's more important to me than any job. I learned people do care. If you treat people the right way, they will respond to you, and I'm talking about the fans from my playing days and the fans who listened on the broadcasts.

They respect me and I respect them. People see me as a normal guy. I'm not afraid to be among them. I go into the inner city, I go places by myself. It's not like the Beatles walking down the street with mobs of people chasing you. They know you, they speak to you. I'll give people a minute to tell their story. My first wife Gladys would say, "Why do you stop and talk to all these people?" And I said, "Because the two minutes you give them now – when you have a bad day – may get you another day they give you down the road." I think people appreciate that they have that one story, that one magical moment where they may have crossed your path. With me, it happens a lot – you try to remember, but you feel good because they remember and want to share it with you. It just reinforces what you are doing and keeps you wanting to do it. In the final count in all of this stuff, when I think about all the people I have worked with, I think I did a decent job. I always try to be genuine. And I hope they appreciated what I did. But there are times now, when I have to wonder if some people in the

19

Royals organization really liked me in the first place. I was as accessible as anyone in the organization. After it all blew up, I received calls from friends, family, fans and work associates saying they were surprised, shocked and disappointed.

A lot of things make me hurt, but I can tell you one thing that doesn't sting. When I look in the mirror now, I see a smiling face looking back at me. And I like that guy in the mirror.

20 "He worked hard to become a Gold Glove third baseman and he was the best clutch hitter in the game."

NOW THAT I HAVE REACHED A MOMENT OF REFLECTION IN MY career, it's time to look back at my all-time Kansas City Royals baseball team. While some choices were easy, a few positions provided quite a challenge.

Let's start with catcher, where I have Darrell Porter. He had a tenacity behind the plate that I really liked. He wasn't afraid to have his pitchers throw inside to protect his teammates and he made our pitching staff as tough as he was. He edges out Jim Sundberg, who was with us a short period of time. He was responsible for bringing along young pitchers like Bret Sabherhagen, Mark Gubicza and Danny Jackson – members of the staff that led us to the World Series championship in 1985. Sunny was the best defensive catcher I was ever around, but Darrell was a much better offensive catcher.

Big John Mayberry is my first baseman. He had soft hands that saved everyone on this team a countless number of errors. He'd always tell us to throw the ball anywhere in front of him and he'd catch it – and he did. And I loved is overall attitude about the game. He told me that you never make excuses on this team, you just go out and get the job done. If you make a mistake admit to it and go back out and keep working hard. Big John could hit – he had a couple of years where he put up some big numbers.

Cookie Rojas taught me a lot about the game. It was tough for a kid from the Royals Academy to replace someone as popular as Cookie. He was a tough guy and he helped me learn how to play second base when he was my manager in winter ball. I'll put Cookie at second, and I think I might be on there, too.

I have a tie at shortstop between Freddie Patek and U.L. Washington. They both brought something special to the game. Freddie had a great arm, but so did U.L., and they both had a toughness around the bag at second base. They brought what I like to call a football mentality to the game. They made my job at second base easier because we all knew what the other guy was thinking. Freddie was also a great base stealer. They were great double play partners.

George Brett and I came up together and it was amazing watching him become one of the greatest players of all time. He worked hard to become a Gold Glove third baseman and he was the best clutch hitter in the game. He ran hard, he broke up double plays, he loved the game and he played it the way it should be played. Watching him go after the .400 batting mark in 1980 was so much fun. He was the best.

Willie Wilson in left field. He was so fast and aggressive and he won a Gold Glove. He worked hard to be a great outfielder, and when Amos Otis was released, he moved to center field and did a great job there,

Big John Mayberry, second from right, and I take some time to visit with these Kansas City police officers. Big John looks like he's having a good time with the police officers and I know that we had to be the two safest guys in Kansas City, surrounded by KC's finest.

too. I think people forget what a great base stealer he was. He led the league in steals and he won a batting title. He didn't have a strong arm, but he had every other tool you'd be looking for in a great ball player.

Amos Otis is my centerfielder. He was the most knowledgeable player I ever played with on the Royals. He made everything look so easy, and that's because he was always in the right position. He didn't make that many difficult plays, because he knew where to play every batter. And he was one of the first Royals to always find a way to get the big hit. He was a complete ballplayer.

Al Cowens was a tough kid from Compton, California, who brought a toughness to this team. He had a great arm and we communicated real well with each other. He could do it all – run, hit, throw – he had a cannon for an arm – and in my entire career I never ran into a right fielder trying to catch a pop fly.

I have five pitchers on my team, and a few selections might surprise some people. My No. 1 pitcher is Steve Busby, who threw a no-hitter each of his first two seasons and who I think would be in the Hall of Fame if he hadn't hurt his arm. Bret Sabeherhagen is No. 2. There was a stretch that began in 1985 – when we won the World Series – that you just knew the team was going to win every time Sabes took the ball to the mound. He was a competitor, but he was a kid who had a lot of fun, too. Dennis Leonard was a guy who wanted to throw a complete game every time he pitched. He didn't like to give the ball up and he was a fierce competitor. He is my No. 3 choice. No. 4 is Paul Splittorff, who wore those glasses and didn't look as tough as he actually was. He was as competitive as Busby and he is the team's all-time winningest pitcher. I bet a lot of fans don't realize that Splitt won more games than anyone else. And No. 5 is Larry Gura, a guy who didn't have great stuff, but knew how to pitch. I always felt comfortable when Larry pitched a big game for us.

My reliever is Dan Quisenberry, who was the best reliever in baseball for about a five or six year period. When Quiz came in from the bullpen, that was it – you knew you'd won.

Hal McRae is my designated hitter. You'd hear a lot of guys say they didn't like the DH position, but Hal embraced it. He would find ways to keep loose and warm between at bats – he might run in the tunnel or go out to the bullpen and he was as competitive as anyone I was ever around. No one ran the bases harder than Hal. I think George watched Hal run the bases and that's why he ran the bases so hard. Hal was a leader in the clubhouse, a no nonsense guy, but no one had more fun playing baseball than Hal.

Picking a manager is tough. Jack McKeon was there for me early in my career, and Whitey Herzog was a great manager, a Hall of Fame manager, who treated his players well. But I have to go with Dick Howser, who saw something in me no other manager saw. When Dick put me in the cleanup spot in the batting order in the 1985 World Series, that showed me he thought I was a complete ballplayer, and that made me a more confident player and a better player.

21 "Do you know that this is the first baseball game played on this field in 35 years?"

I enjoyed a special moment this past summer when a special place from my childhood became a gathering point for young baseball players today.

As volunteers piled charcoal on a grill, and tables and chairs were placed in a shelter house, Frank White stood near a makeshift dugout and watched as youngsters looked for missing belts, gloves and hats while parents and coaches did their best to organize a few pregame activities at Spring Valley Park. Memories, like the glowing sun that bathed the meticulous playing field in a golden hue, washed over Frank as he thought back to the days when he and his best friend, Leon Slaughter, ruled the diamonds located at 28th and Brooklyn, in the heart of downtown Kansas City.

"Do you know that this is the first baseball game played on this field in over 35 years?" asked the Kansas City Royals Hall of Fame second baseman, as the Missouri Diamond Masters played the Kansas City Varsity Sports RBI (Reviving Baseball in the Inner-city) team. "What the Key Coalition and Kansas City Parks and Recreation Department have done with this park and the surrounding area is just amazing. "I never played an organized game here, but this is where Leon and I would come as soon as our chores were done. And we'd play until dark, and get home. This was our second home – actually, we probably spent more time here than we did at our real home."

For decades, White's former playground became a gathering point for junkies and drug dealers. It was an eyesore and an embarrassment to the hard working people who still called the inner city home. So they decided to do something about it. Now, the umpire's call of, "Play ball!" resonates throughout Spring Valley Park. And the man who inspired the community to re-name the baseball field Frank White Jr., Field, was on hand to take part in the festivities. It was a bright Saturday morning that featured two 10 and under RBI teams in a game that became the main attraction of the Key Coalition Family Fun Day at the park. "We have a very special partnership with the Parks and Recreation Department," said Key Coalition spokesperson Karen Slaughter, whose husband Leon is White's longtime friend. "Today, we have young men playing baseball in the park where Frank played as a youngster and we hope he will serve as an inspiration for them to grow into the type citizens we can all be proud of. We're just so honored to not only have Frank here today, but to still have his presence in our community.

Mark Bowland, the manager of community services for the Parks and Recreation Department said that Saturday morning at Spring Valley Park was a day he will always remember. "This is one of the greatest days in the history of the Kansas City Parks and Recreation Department," Bowland said. "We're taking our parks back, we're pushing out the negative elements and replacing them with the youngsters who are the future of our city. We're witnessing a baseball game here today, but this is a game that will make a difference - a positive difference - in our community." Frank threw out the ceremonial first pitch and visited with the members of each team, but he refused to take any credit for the renaissance of the park and the surrounding area. "All the credit goes to Karen and the Key Coalition Committee," Frank said. "They pushed for the change, they did all the things you need to do to complete a project like this. And I'm proud to have my name associated with it." As the youngsters played and a picnic *area was beginning to fill with members of the community, two KCMO police officers watched the youngsters play from a vantage point in center field. "I bet they're enjoying today," an elderly fan said, pointing in the direction of the officers. "They probably had to deal with some bad things in this park. But thankfully, those days are over now, we can all come out and just watch the kids play baseball – like we used to do when Frank was a young man playing in this park." A gentleman in a crisp white shirt and baseball cap nodded in agreement. It was Don Motley, the former Ban Johnson League manager and one of the founders of the Negro Leagues Baseball Museum, who watched Frank and his friends play in this setting more than four decades ago. "We all knew Frank was special," Motley said, "but I don't know if any of us knew he was going to be the great player he became. But I'm even prouder that he became a great man. They only name parks after great men – and there's Frank's name on that sign on the backstop. I always knew he was a great man – and now, everyone else will know, too."*

Kids relaxing at home. (left to right) Terrance, Courtney, Adrianne, and Frank III.

22 Frankly Speaking

I have always had a special relationship with my fans, friends and teammates. Here are a few special stories we wanted to share with you. I hope you enjoy them as much I did when I read them for the first time.

FRANK WHITE

On August 16, 1973, I attended my first professional baseball game: Evansville Triplets v. Omaha Royals at Rosenblatt Stadium. This was a big deal for a small town Iowa boy. Like every 11 year old, I was eager to gain a few autographs prior to the first pitch. I grabbed a pen, my official game day program (35 cents ... still have it) and made my way down to the Royals dugout. I stood against the rail at the far end of the dugout too petrified to say anything to the players. After a few minutes, which seemed like hours to me, one player (who was engaged in a conversation with another fan) made his way down to me, reached up and signed my program. I mumbled a couple words that may have sounded like, "Thank you." Who knows ... but I had my first autograph! That player was Frank White. Frank walked back to the other end of the dugout and continued his conversation. I remember hearing the fan say, "We will see you up there (KC) soon."

Yes ... we sure did.

MIKE THEOBALD

My fondest memory of Frank White comes from about 1994. I would have been about 14 years old and of course eager to work on my game to prepare me for the big leagues. My dad registered me for a Frank White Baseball Day Camp at Pink Hill Park in Blue Springs. My excitement grew each day as that Saturday drew closer. I got new batting gloves and cleats for the camp, and that night I slept with my glove. That morning the tears streamed down my face harder than the rain that flooded the streets and the fields we were supposed to play on. We got there and Frank offered to either refund the fee or, we could stay and we would make do. There couldn't have been 7 or 8 of us that decided to stay and take instruction. Frank and his entire group stayed and gave one on one instruction to each of us. He could have left, but he stayed through the whole day and spent lots of time with each of us. Even as a youngster I remember thinking how unusual it was that big time instructors and players would stay and spend time with such few of us. I really appreciated that day, Frank. That day began the respect and appreciation that I have for this wonderful gem that we here in Kansas City have in Frank White.

BRENDAN WILLIAMS

I was born in 1965 and since I was a little kid my grandmother would always take me to Royals games. Those were some of my earliest memories. I was lucky to be growing up when the Royals were becoming a great team and I got to enjoy all of the memories - many heartbreaking - but many more were wonderful. From the end-of-the-world losses to the Yankees in the playoffs in '76, '77 and '78 to the revenge of finally beating them in '80 Then of course the awesome come-from behind victories over the Blue Jays and Cardinals in '85. Through all of those times my favorite player was always and still is Frank White. I was always a fan of effortless, smooth players and great defense and there was never a better example than Frank White. I've always been impressed with how classy he is and how he handled everything. He was truly a great person to have as a role model growing up. After the great run in 1985 with Frank batting clean-up in the World Series, I was lucky enough to see him voted to another All-Star Game in 1986. Even better, it was on my 21st birthday, July 15, 1986. I went to the Longbranch Saloon with my mother and my grandmother to celebrate my birthday and we got to watch the game together just like when I was a kid, only this time in a bar, with a beer. How many guys spent their 21st birthday in a bar with their mother and grandmother? But for me it was the best. I wouldn't have it any other way. The game was close and the American League was up 2-0 in the later part of the game when Frank came in to pinch hit against Mike Scott. He was pitching in his hometown ball park and the crowd was going crazy. The National League had been dominating the game for many years so it was really exciting for us to be leading. Frank got behind in the count 0-2 and then he hit the next pitch for a home run to left center. The whole bar went crazy. It ended up being the game-winning run as the National League scored two runs but the American League held on for the victory breaking their streak. It was the best birthday present. Telling you this story sent a chill down my spine just as it did then. Thanks for letting me share it with you.

PS: My entire family took my grandmother to the Royals game this year on June 12th to celebrate her 100th birthday. The Royals announced it to the entire crowd and they all sang happy birthday to her and she got to see it all on the giant scoreboard. Then we beat Milwaukee and Zack Greinke. Another great Royals birthday memory.

SCOTT CLAYPOOL

I was with my wife and son at First Watch restaurant in independence. Frank came over and sat with my family for at least 15 minutes just like he was a friend of the family. What an incredible person who cares about Kansas City and who is very humble!!! I am so disappointed with the Royals for pushing him out! Frank White is Kansas City!

CHAD MEYER

Coming from a guy who grew up going to junior and senior high school with Frank Jr., and playing second base on tournament teams, my favorite Frank White memories came from his spectacular plays. The way he would leap in the air to catch a line drive and then his effortless approach to backhanding a grounder up the middle, jumping and throwing to first to get the runner. That's the one I always tried to copy without any luck. He is the greatest second baseman I have ever seen.

TOM CLARK

I have since had the great opportunity to meet Frank White at Royals Fantasy Camp and speak to him several times since, but two meetings that occurred prior to him knowing who I was stand out. Last year my wife and I went to Boston for a Royals series. We got to the park early and it started raining. Frank was on his way from the dugout to the press box when I saw him and said hi. We spoke for 15 or 20 seconds, then he said "It might be a long night" and went on his way. Not only was he right about the long night (the game went 13 innings and finished well after midnight) I later saw the broadcast that showed my wife and me on TV, and Frank mentioned that I was a season ticket holder and planned to stay for the whole game no matter what. From just a few seconds conversation hours earlier from a random fan, Frank was able to recognize me and share our conversation. That always impressed me. That is one of the reasons he will always be a fan favorite. When I was a kid in Topeka in the late 1970s early 1980s, Frank would join the Royals caravan and come to a strip mall across from our house just about every year. The strip mall also had a department store that sold baseballs which we used for our daily neighborhood games. The balls were cheap and ended up egg shaped after a few hits. As it was all I had, I took those same balls to Frank and he would always gladly sign them. I wish I could have read his mind when he saw those deformed dirty baseballs.

DAVE DARBY

For 41 years I have been with KMDO-AM @ KOMB-FM in Fort Scott, Kan., about 90 miles south of Kansas City. I had the opportunity in the 1970s and 1980s to interview Frank several times in the Royals clubhouse after games. While most of the players of that era were friendly and cooperative, Frank was even more so. Frank never turned me down for an interview. He answered all of my questions with grace. I remember one time in 1978 when I was talking to Frank. After that interview, I mentioned to Frank that our station was holding an auction to benefit a local charity and asked if he could donate anything to the charity. I was hoping for an autographed picture. Instead, Frank gave me his game used Royals hat and he autographed the bill. Now this happened in June or July of that season at a time when the team only issued two or three hats to a player per year. This is the kind of man Frank White is. I remember Al Zych, the equipment manager at the time, gave me a couple of broken bats, but Frank's hat was the highlight of the auction. Not only was Frank White a great player, he is a great gentleman.

GARY WEBSTER

I lockered next to Frank for five years. Well, I actually lockered next to an empty locker because Frank had two lockers – which gave me the opportunity to steal a bat here and there when he wasn't looking (laughs). But that wasn't the first time I was around Frank. I was in college and we played against the Academy team, and back then you could tell which players had the chance to make it the big leagues and Frank was one of them. It's an honor to call him my friend and we shared some great times over the five years we were teammates. Smooth's Corner, which was the name of the corner of the locker room where Frank had his two lockers, was a great place to be. I never heard a cross word from Frank during those five years. We became close friends and still are today.

GREG PRYOR

My brother, U.L. played with Frank and I knew he was a great player, but now, after being around him and seeing how much he cares for his community, I know he is a great man. He wants Kansas City to be special. He lives here and he does so much for the community, for the kids – for all of us. The RBI Program wouldn't be as successful as it is today without Frank, and you can talk to anyone associated with it and they will tell you that Frank White was a godsend to the program and this community.

JAMES WASHINGTON

Credibility, class, and dedication to the community – these are words that best describe Frank White, Jr. Frank gets my nomination as a genuine hometown hero! My wife and I have been fans of Frank since he emerged on the horizon with the Kansas City Royals, replacing the very popular Cookie Rojas at second base. As his professional career developed, it became an ever increasing pleasure to watch Frank glide around second base, making even the most difficult plays seem routine. Validating our opinion of Frank, through his years at second base with the Royals, Frank earned a Gold Glove Award eight times, and in our and popular opinion, he should have won that award a ninth time! Despite Frank's superior statistics, sadly, Harold Reynolds won the Gold Glove Award that year. When Frank White first joined the broadcasting team at Fox Sports/Kansas City, my family and I enjoyed his occasional, on-air, color commentary of each K.C. Royals game. In general, he was in a support position at first, assisting Paul Splittorff, and substituting for Paul when he was absent. And, at some point prior to Paul's death, Frank took over as the color commentator. My wife and I relished in that decision! Frank was (and is) incredibly knowledgeable about major league baseball, and especially the Kansas City Royals. And he was not reticent to share that knowledge, including the details of playing the various positions on the field, with all the viewers. Unlike many former athletes, Frank is not just knowledgeable, but also extremely articulate. In 2006, at my age 63, I became totally disabled with a series of diseases. So, I became even more directed toward sports on TV, especially baseball and the Kansas City Royals. And when Frank came on the scene of Fox Sports/Kansas City, he did such a superior job of handling color commentary that I sent numerous supportive letters to both administrative personnel at the Kansas City Royals organization and to Fox Sports/Kansas City, complimenting them on their choice of Frank as their color commentator for the K.C. Royals broadcasts. Obviously, as was the case with many, many fans of those broadcasts, I was incredibly disappointed and depressed to learn that last December, Frank was fired. Besides Frank's obvious talent as color commentator for Fox Sports/Kansas City, he has continued to be highly visible with various area charities, causes, and venues. He has devoted a substantial amount of his time to supporting causes like the American Cancer Society, the Quit Smoking Campaign, the Kansas City Zoo, and many, many others --- and he continues to do so. At one previous point, after sending one of my congratulatory letters to the K.C. Royals about Frank, I got a direct call from Frank, thanking me for my support. I was "stunned" that a highly visible sports personality like Frank would take the time make a personal call to me. But, knowing him now as I do, I shouldn't have been surprised. What a real gentleman he is! Since that time, we have communicated back-and-forth regarding various issues. I might add that after my relatively recent period of hospitalization, both Frank and his wife Teresa called my home to see how my recovery was going. Can you name any other sports personality who would take the time to do that? I require externally provided oxygen 24/7, and as such it is very difficult for me to venture very far outside our home. But, Frank and Teresa have invited my wife and me to be their guest at any future Kansas City T-Bones game, where Frank is the first base coach. As soon as the weather becomes more manageable, we plan to take them up on that offer.

DREW J. DIETERICH

Frank and I have been good friends for over 30 years and have had some good times. I recall a time when Frank was doing an autograph session in Harrisonville, Mo., prior to a big sports auction. I disguised myself as an old man with a cane. I got into the line and waited my turn until Frank greeted me. I handed him several items to autograph. I disguised my voice and said that I was his biggest fan. In a typical Frank White style, he was appreciative of my comments. I told him I was at The K and watched him pitch his first perfect game. Frank, being very proper, did not want to embarrass me. He thought I had confused him with someone else. I told him that I also remember at The K when he made an outstanding catch in center field robbing Reggie Jackson of a home run. Again, he was being very nice to tell me that it must have been someone else and that he had never played center field. At this time, Frank is probably thinking that this old man has dementia. I then take my disguise off and say, "I got you." Everybody breaks out in laughter. Frank says a few choice words and then breaks into laughter.

DICK LACY

I can say with a great deal of pride that I was once Frank White's teammate. And I am sure that I remember the game a lot more than Frank, because it took place at old Municipal Stadium when we were teenagers. I played for Bell Pest from Independence and Frank played for Safeway. It was the Casey Stengel League All-Star Game and back then you could tell that Frank was going to be something special. We were a bunch of teenagers and it was interesting watching the way the players approached the game. Frank just had so much poise and you could tell – way back then – that he was going to be a special player. And getting to talk with him, you could tell he was a great young man. I've had the pleasure of meeting with Frank many times over the years and he hasn't changed a bit. He is the class of the class.

TIM CRONE

Fans used to say that I was smooth when I played for the Royals. But there was only one "SMOOTH" player on the Royals – and that was Frank.

AMOS OTIS

When I first met Frank, I was 26 and it was so exciting that he and my mother were getting married. He is a great man -- a great, great man. When my youngest children see him on TV they talk to him and say, 'Big Daddy, Big Daddy!' and they wonder why he doesn't talk back to them. They love him so much - we all do. Over the past 11 years, he's given me an inside look into the world of baseball. I've seen him and George Brett and Willie Wilson and some other players in their element. It's fascinating. We now live in Arizona, so we don't see him as much as we used to, but we still love to visit with him and his grand kids love him so much. We were there for his statue unveiling and so many other wonderful things in his life like coaching and working on TV. We are blessed to have him as a part of our family.

MICHAEL WILLIAMS
Frank White's step-son, who is a warehouse manager
for QuikTrip in Arizona

23 "Never say never."

I WAS A BIG TOPIC OF DISCUSSION IN KANSAS CITY RIGHT AFTER I was fired and during the All-Star Game. I did a lot of interviews. I even said earlier in this book that I would never step foot inside Kauffman Stadium again. Then, I remembered something that Tony Muser said to me, and I wish I could have remembered it right before I made that statement about never going back to the stadium again. He said, "Never say never. Never say always. What's most important is to be right at that particular time." So, I guess anything is possible. But I think that in order to get over something you have to get away from it. It is like a divorce. You don't keep going over to her house and saying, "Oh baby please." I can't do that. If you know something is broken and you don't feel like it can be repaired right away, just get away from it. You may need to step away, just to have a chance to get better. Will I step back in that stadium?

Never say never.

24 My Career Stats

Frank White Hitting Statistics

Year	Age	Games	AB	R	H	2B	3B	HR	GRSL	RBI
1973	23	51	139	20	31	6	1	0	0	5
1974	24	99	204	19	45	6	3	1	0	18
1975	25	111	304	43	76	10	2	7	1	36
1976	26	152	446	39	102	17	6	2	0	46
1977	27	152	474	59	116	21	5	5	0	50
1978	28	143	461	66	127	24	6	7	0	50
1979	29	127	467	73	124	26	4	10	0	48
1980	30	154	560	70	148	23	4	7	0	60
1981	31	94	364	35	91	17	1	9	1	38
1982	32	145	524	71	156	45	6	11	0	56
1983	33	146	549	52	143	35	6	11	0	77
1984	34	129	479	58	130	22	5	17	1	56
1985	35	149	563	62	140	25	1	22	1	69
1986	36	151	566	76	154	37	3	22	1	84
1987	37	154	563	67	138	32	2	17	1	78
1988	38	150	537	48	126	25	1	8	0	58
1989	39	135	418	34	107	22	1	2	0	36
1990	40	82	241	20	52	14	1	2	0	21
18 Yrs		2324	7859	912	2006	407	58	160	6	886

BB	IBB	SO	SH	SF	HBP	GIDP	AVG	OBP	SLG
8	0	23	2	2	0	1	.223	.262	.281
5	0	33	5	0	0	4	.221	.239	.294
20	0	39	2	2	1	4	.250	.297	.365
19	0	42	18	3	3	4	.229	.263	.307
25	0	67	11	2	2	4	.245	.284	.342
26	1	59	9	2	3	2	.275	.317	.399
25	3	54	3	7	1	11	.266	.300	.403
19	0	69	9	4	2	11	.264	.289	.357
19	0	50	4	3	0	10	.250	.285	.376
16	1	65	7	5	2	12	.298	.318	.469
20	4	51	4	6	0	18	.260	.283	.406
27	3	72	4	3	2	11	.271	.311	.445
28	2	86	5	3	1	8	.249	.284	.414
43	5	88	2	7	2	10	.272	.322	.465
51	5	86	4	4	2	16	.245	.308	.400
21	3	67	7	6	4	16	.235	.266	.330
30	0	52	5	3	2	7	.256	.307	.328
10	0	32	0	3	3	7	.216	.253	.307
412	**27**	**1035**	**101**	**65**	**30**	**156**	**.255**	**.293**	**.383**

Frank White Fielding Statistics

YEAR	POS	G	GS	TC	TC/G	CH	PO
1973	2B	11	10	62	5.6	59	19
1973	SS	37	23	142	3.8	133	52
1974	2B	50	25	157	3.1	151	67
1974	3B	16	10	51	2.6	39	15
1974	SS	29	17	122	4.2	118	37
1975	2B	67	57	307	4.6	303	124
1975	3B	4	2	8	2	8	1
1975	C	1	-	6	6	5	2
1975	SS	42	26	148	3.5	141	55
1976	2B	130	122	665	5.1	647	256
1976	SS	37	20	138	3.7	133	41
1977	2B	152	145	752	4.9	744	310
1977	SS	4	1	3	0.8	3	0
1978	2B	140	138	726	5.2	710	325
1979	2B	125	125	661	5.3	649	317
1980	2B	153	145	853	5.6	843	395
1981	2B	93	93	495	5.3	489	226
1982	2B	144	143	767	5.3	750	361
1983	2B	145	142	840	5.8	832	390
1984	2B	129	126	735	5.7	724	299
1985	2B	149	147	849	5.7	832	342
1986	2B	151	144	765	5.1	755	316
1986	3B	1	0	0	0	0	0
1986	SS	1	0	3	3	3	1
1987	2B	152	150	788	5.2	778	320
1988	2B	148	139	723	4.9	719	293
1989	2B	132	126	655	5	645	238
1989	CF	1	-	0	0	0	0
1990	2B	79	75	368	4.7	360	142
1990	RF	1	0	6	6	0	0

A	E	DP	PB	CASB	CACS	FLD%
40	3	12	n/a	n/a	n/a	0.952
81	9	24	n/a	n/a	n/a	0.937
84	6	23	n/a	n/a	n/a	0.962
24	2	1	n/a	n/a	n/a	0.951
81	4	16	n/a	n/a	n/a	0.967
179	4	35	n/a	n/a	n/a	0.987
7	0	1	n/a	n/a	n/a	1
3	1	0	0	-	-	0.833
86	7	20	n/a	n/a	n/a	0.953
391	18	76	n/a	n/a	n/a	0.973
92	5	14	n/a	n/a	n/a	0.964
434	8	86	n/a	n/a	n/a	0.989
3	0	0	n/a	n/a	n/a	1
385	16	96	n/a	n/a	n/a	0.978
332	12	78	n/a	n/a	n/a	0.982
448	10	103	n/a	n/a	n/a	0.988
263	6	70	n/a	n/a	n/a	0.988
389	17	99	n/a	n/a	n/a	0.978
442	8	123	n/a	n/a	n/a	0.990
425	11	97	n/a	n/a	n/a	0.985
490	17	101	n/a	n/a	n/a	0.980
439	10	91	n/a	n/a	n/a	0.987
0	0	0	n/a	n/a	n/a	0
2	0	1	n/a	n/a	n/a	1
458	10	89	n/a	n/a	n/a	0.987
426	4	88	n/a	n/a	n/a	0.994
407	10	64	n/a	n/a	n/a	0.985
0	0	0	n/a	n/a	n/a	0
218	8	51	n/a	n/a	n/a	0.978
0	0	0	n/a	n/a	n/a	0

Frank White Fielding Statistics: Career Totals

YEAR	G	GS	TC	TC/G	CH	PO
2B Totals	2150	2052	11,168	5.2	10,990	4,740
SS Totals	150	87	556	3.7	531	186
3B Totals	21	12	49	2.3	47	16
RF Totals	1	0	0	0.0	0	0
CF Totals	1	0	0	0.0	0	0
C Totals	1	0	6	6.0	5	2
18 Years	2,332	2,151	11,779	5.1	11,573	4,944

A	E	DP	PB	CASB	CACS	FLD%
6,250	178	1,382	n/a	n/a	n/a	.984
345	25	75	n/a	n/a	n/a	.955
31	2	2	n/a	n/a	n/a	.959
0	0	0	n/a	n/a	n/a	.000
0	0	0	n/a	n/a	n/a	.000
3	1	0	0	n/a	n/a	.833
6,629	206	1,459	0	n/a	n/a	.983

"Baseball is a difficult game to learn and we put much of our resources into the offensive side of the game, when the beauty and grace of the game comes from the good fundamentals of base running and playing defense."

1985 World Series Box Scores

Game 1

St. Louis Cardinals 3, Kansas City Royals 1

At Royals Stadium

Game played on Saturday, October 19, 1985 at Royals Stadium

St. Louis Cardinals	ab	r	h	rbi	Kansas City Royals	ab	r	h	rbi
McGee cf	4	0	1	1	Smith lf	3	0	1	0
Smith ss	3	0	0	0	Wilson cf	4	0	1	0
Herr 2b	4	1	1	0	Brett 3b	4	0	1	0
Clark 1b	4	0	1	1	White 2b	4	0	0	0
Landrum lf	4	1	2	0	Sundberg c	3	1	1	0
Cedeno rf	3	0	1	1	Motley rf	3	0	1	0
Worrell p	1	0	0	0	Sheridan ph	1	0	1	0
Pendleton 3b	2	1	0	0	Balboni 1b	4	0	1	1
Porter c	3	0	1	0	Biancalana ss	1	0	0	0
Tudor p	1	0	0	0	Jones ph	1	0	1	0
Van Slyke rf	2	0	0	0	Quisenberry p	0	0	0	0
Totals	31	3	7	3	Black p	0	0	0	0
					Orta ph	1	0	0	0
					Jackson p	2	0	0	0
					McRae ph	0	0	0	0
					Concepcion pr,ss	0	0	0	0
					Iorg ph	1	0	0	0
					Totals	32	1	8	1

St. Louis	0	0	1	1	0	0	0	0	1	–	3	7	1
Kansas City	0	1	0	0	0	0	0	0	0	–	1	8	0

St. Louis Cardinals	IP	H	R	ER	BB	SO
Tudor W (1-0)	6.2	7	1	1	2	5
Worrell SV (1)	2.1	1	0	0	1	0
Totals	9.0	8	1	1	3	5

Kansas City Royals	IP	H	R	ER	BB	SO
Jackson L (0-1)	7.0	4	2	2	2	7
Quisenberry	1.2	3	1	1	0	2
Black	0.1	0	0	0	2	1
Totals	9.0	7	3	3	4	10

E–Pendleton (1). DP–St. Louis 1. PB–Sundberg (1). 2B–St. Louis Landrum (1,off Jackson); Cedeno (1,off Jackson); McGee (1,off Jackson); Clark (1,off Quisenberry), Kansas City Sundberg (1,off Tudor); Sheridan (1,off Worrell). 3B–Kansas City Jones (1,off Tudor). SH–Tudor (1,off Jackson). IBB–Pendleton (1,by Black). HBP–McRae (1,by Tudor). SB–Smith (1,2nd base off Jackson/Sundberg). CS–Motley (1,Home by Tudor/Porter); Smith (1,2nd base by Tudor/Porter). HBP–Tudor (1,McRae). IBB–Black (1,Pendleton). U–Don Denkinger (AL), Bill Williams (NL), Jim McKean (AL), Bob Engel (NL), Jim Quick (NL), John Shulock (AL). T–2:48. A–41,650.

1985 World Series Box Scores

Game 2

St. Louis Cardinals 4, Kansas City Royals 2

At Royals Stadium

Game played on Sunday, October 20, 1985 at Royals Stadium

St. Louis Cardinals	ab	r	h	rbi	Kansas City Royals	ab	r	h	rbi
McGee cf	4	1	1	0	Smith lf	4	0	2	0
Smith ss	4	0	0	0	Jones lf	0	0	0	0
Herr 2b	4	0	0	0	Wilson cf	4	1	2	0
Clark 1b	3	1	1	1	Brett 3b	4	1	1	1
Landrum lf	4	1	2	0	White 2b	3	0	3	1
Cedeno rf	3	1	0	0	Sheridan rf	4	0	0	0
Lahti p	0	0	0	0	Quisenberry p	0	0	0	0
Pendleton 3b	4	0	2	3	Sundberg c	4	0	0	0
Porter c	3	0	0	0	Balboni 1b	4	0	1	0
Cox p	2	0	0	0	Biancalana ss	1	0	0	0
Harper ph	1	0	0	0	Orta ph	1	0	0	0
Dayley p	0	0	0	0	Leibrandt p	2	0	0	0
Van Slyke ph,rf	1	0	0	0	Motley rf	0	0	0	0
Totals	33	4	6	4	Totals	31	2	9	2

St. Louis	0	0	0		0	0	0		0	0	4	–	4	6	0
Kansas City	0	0	0		2	0	0		0	0	0	–	2	9	0

St. Louis Cardinals	IP	H	R	ER	BB	SO
Cox	7.0	7	2	2	3	5
Dayley W (1-0)	1.0	1	0	0	0	1
Lahti SV (1)	1.0	1	0	0	0	0
Totals	9.0	9	2	2	3	6

Kansas City Royals	IP	H	R	ER	BB	SO
Leibrandt L (0-1)	8.2	6	4	4	2	6
Quisenberry	0.1	0	0	0	1	0
Totals	9.0	6	4	4	3	6

E–None. DP–St. Louis 3. 2B–St. Louis McGee (2,off Leibrandt); Landrum (2,off Leibrandt); Pendleton (1,off Leibrandt), Kansas City Brett (1,off Cox); White 2 (2,off Cox,off Dayley). IBB–Cedeno (1,by Leibrandt); Porter (1,by Quisenberry). SH–Leibrandt (1,off Cox). SB–White (1,2nd base off Cox/Porter); Wilson (1,2nd base off Cox/Porter). IBB–Leibrandt (1,Cedeno); Quisenberry (1,Porter). U–Bill Williams (NL), Jim McKean (AL), Bob Engel (NL), John Shulock (AL), Don Denkinger (AL), Jim Quick (NL). T–2:44. A–41,656.

"In the lust for good offense some things in the game are overlooked, such as bunting, hitting in game situations and base running."

1985 World Series Box Scores

Game 3

Kansas City Royals 6, St. Louis Cardinals 1

At Busch Stadium

Game played on Tuesday, October 22, 1985 at Busch Stadium

Kansas City Royals	ab	r	h	rbi	St. Louis Cardinals	ab	r	h	rbi
Smith lf	5	0	2	2	McGee cf	4	0	1	0
Jones lf	0	0	0	0	Smith ss	4	1	1	0
Wilson cf	5	0	2	0	Herr 2b	3	0	1	0
Brett 3b	2	2	2	0	Clark 1b	4	0	1	1
White 2b	4	2	2	3	Van Slyke rf	4	0	0	0
Sheridan rf	5	0	0	0	Pendleton 3b	4	0	1	0
Sundberg c	2	1	1	0	Porter c	3	0	0	0
Balboni 1b	4	0	0	0	Landrum lf	3	0	1	0
Biancalana ss	5	1	2	1	Andujar p	1	0	0	0
Saberhagen p	3	0	0	0	Campbell p	0	0	0	0
Totals	35	6	11	6	Jorgensen ph	1	0	0	0
					Horton p	0	0	0	0
					Harper ph	1	0	0	0
					Dayley p	0	0	0	0
					Totals	32	1	6	1

Kansas City	0	0	0	2	2	0	2	0	0	–	6	11	0
St. Louis	0	0	0	0	0	1	0	0	0	–	1	6	0

Kansas City Royals	IP	H	R	ER	BB	SO
Saberhagen W (1-0)	9.0	6	1	1	1	8
Totals	9.0	6	1	1	1	8

St. Louis Cardinals	IP	H	R	ER	BB	SO
Andujar L (0-1)	4.0	9	4	4	3	3
Campbell	1.0	0	0	0	1	2
Horton	2.0	2	2	2	2	1
Dayley	2.0	0	0	0	2	2
Totals	9.0	11	6	6	8	8

E–None. **DP**–Kansas City 1, St. Louis 1. **2B**–Kansas City Smith (1,off Andujar); White (3,off Horton). **HR**–Kansas City White (1,5th inning off Andujar 1 on, 0 out). **SH**–Saberhagen (1,off Andujar). **IBB**–Brett (1,by Andujar); Balboni (1,by Horton). **SB**–Wilson (2,2nd base off Andujar/Porter); McGee (1,2nd base off Saberhagen/Sundberg). **CS**–Smith (2,2nd base by Andujar/Porter); McGee (1,3rd base by Saberhagen/Sundberg). **BK**–Horton (1). **IBB**–Andujar (1,Brett); Horton (1,Balboni). **U**–Jim McKean (AL), Bob Engel (NL), John Shulock (AL), Jim Quick (NL), Bill Williams (NL), Don Denkinger (AL). **T**–2:59. **A**–53,634.

1985 World Series Box Scores

Game 4

St. Louis Cardinals 3, Kansas City Royals 0

At Busch Stadium

Game played on Wednesday, October 23, 1985 at Busch Stadium

Kansas City Royals	ab	r	h	rbi	St. Louis Cardinals	ab	r	h	rbi
Smith lf	4	0	0	0	McGee cf	3	1	2	1
Wilson cf	4	0	1	0	Smith ss	2	0	0	0
Brett 3b	4	0	1	0	Herr 2b	3	0	1	0
White 2b	4	0	0	0	Clark 1b	3	0	1	0
Sundberg c	4	0	1	0	Landrum lf	4	1	1	1
Motley rf	4	0	0	0	Cedeno rf	3	0	0	0
Balboni 1b	2	0	1	0	Van Slyke rf	0	0	0	0
Biancalana ss	2	0	0	0	Pendleton 3b	3	1	1	0
McRae ph	1	0	0	0	Nieto c	1	0	0	1
Concepcion ss	0	0	0	0	Tudor p	3	0	0	0
Black p	1	0	0	0	Totals	25	3	6	3
Wathan ph	1	0	0	0					
Beckwith p	0	0	0	0					
Jones ph	1	0	1	0					
Quisenberry p	0	0	0	0					
Totals	32	0	5	0					

Kansas City	0	0	0		0	0	0		0	0	0	–	0	5	1
St. Louis	0	1	1		0	1	0		0	0	x	–	3	6	0

Kansas City Royals	IP	H	R	ER	BB	SO
Black L (0-1)	5.0	4	3	3	3	3
Beckwith	2.0	1	0	0	0	3
Quisenberry	1.0	1	0	0	2	0
Totals	8.0	6	3	3	5	6

St. Louis Cardinals	IP	H	R	ER	BB	SO
Tudor W (2-0)	9.0	5	0	0	1	8
Totals	9.0	5	0	0	1	8

E–Black (1). DP-Kansas City 1. 2B-Kansas City Jones (1,off Tudor), St. Louis Herr (1,off Beckwith). 3B–St. Louis Pendleton (1,off Black). HR–St. Louis Landrum (1,2nd inning off Black 0 on, 1 out); McGee (1,3rd inning off Black 0 on, 2 out). SH–Nieto (1,off Black). SB–Smith (1,off Quisenberry). IBB–McGee (1,by Black); Herr (1,by Quisenberry). CS–Smith (1,2nd base by Black/Sundberg) WP–Quisenberry (1). IBB–Black (2,McGee); Quisenberry (2,Herr). U–Bob Engel (NL), John Shulock (AL), Jim Quick (NL), Don Denkinger (AL), Jim McKean (AL), Bill Williams (NL). T–2:19. A–53,634.

"I just wanted people to remember that things can get tough and things may not go your way. That's just part of life. But also remember that you are somebody. Be true to yourself. Respect and love yourself. In the end, you only have your name."

1985 World Series Box Scores

Game 5

Kansas City Royals 6, St. Louis Cardinals 1

At Busch Stadium

Game played on Thursday, October 24, 1985 at Busch Stadium

Kansas City Royals	ab	r	h	rbi	St. Louis Cardinals	ab	r	h	rbi
Smith lf	4	2	2	0	McGee cf	4	0	2	0
Jones lf	0	0	0	0	Smith ss	3	0	0	0
Wilson cf	5	0	2	2	Herr 2b	4	1	1	0
Brett 3b	4	0	1	0	Clark 1b	3	0	1	1
Pryor 3b	0	0	0	0	Landrum lf	4	0	1	0
White 2b	5	1	0	1	Cedeno rf	4	0	0	0
Sheridan rf	5	0	2	1	Pendleton 3b	3	0	0	0
Balboni 1b	4	0	1	0	Nieto c	4	0	0	0
Sundberg c	4	2	1	0	Forsch p	0	0	0	0
Biancalana ss	3	1	2	1	Horton p	1	0	0	0
Jackson p	4	0	0	0	Campbell p	0	0	0	0
Totals	38	6	11	5	DeJesus ph	1	0	0	0
					Worrell p	0	0	0	0
					Harper ph	1	0	0	0
					Lahti p	0	0	0	0
					Totals	32	1	5	1

Kansas City	1	3	0	0	0	0	0	1	1	–	6	11	2
St. Louis	1	0	0	0	0	0	0	0	0	–	1	5	1

Kansas City Royals	IP	H	R	ER	BB	SO
Jackson W (1-1)	9.0	5	1	1	3	5
Totals	9.0	5	1	1	3	5

St. Louis Cardinals	IP	H	R	ER	BB	SO
Forsch L (0-1)	1.2	5	4	4	1	2
Horton	2.0	1	0	0	3	4
Campbell	1.1	0	0	0	0	2
Worrell	2.0	0	0	0	0	6
Lahti	2.0	5	2	1	0	1
Totals	9.0	11	6	5	4	15

E–Brett (1), Jackson (1), Smith (1). **DP**–St. Louis 1. **2B**–Kansas City Sundberg (2,off Forsch); Sheridan (2,off Lahti), St. Louis Herr (2,off Jackson); Clark (2,off Jackson). **3B**–Kansas City Wilson (1,off Forsch). **IBB**–Brett (2,by Horton). **SB**–Smith (1,2nd base off Horton/Nieto). **CS**–McGee (2,2nd base by Jackson/Sundberg). **IBB**–Horton (2,Brett). **U**–John Shulock (AL), Jim Quick (NL), Don Denkinger (AL), Bill Williams (NL), Bob Engel (NL), Jim McKean (AL). **T**–2:52. **A**–53,634.

1985 World Series Box Scores

Game 6

Kansas City Royals 2, St. Louis Cardinals 1

At Royals Stadium

Game played on Saturday, October 26, 1985 at Royals Stadium

St. Louis Cardinals	ab	r	h	rbi
Smith ss	3	0	0	0
McGee cf	4	0	0	0
Herr 2b	4	0	0	0
Clark 1b	4	0	0	0
Landrum lf	4	0	1	0
Pendleton 3b	4	1	1	0
Cedeno rf	2	0	1	0
Van Slyke pr,rf	0	0	0	0
Porter c	3	0	1	0
Cox p	2	0	0	0
Harper ph	1	0	1	1
Lawless pr	0	0	0	0
Dayley p	0	0	0	0
Worrell p	0	0	0	0
Totals	31	1	5	1

Kansas City Royals	ab	r	h	rbi
Smith lf	4	0	1	0
Wilson cf	3	0	1	0
Brett 3b	4	0	0	0
White 2b	4	0	1	0
Sheridan rf	3	0	1	0
Motley ph	0	0	0	0
Orta ph	1	0	1	0
Balboni 1b	3	0	2	0
Concepcion pr	0	1	0	0
Sundberg c	4	1	1	0
Biancalana ss	3	0	1	0
McRae ph	0	0	0	0
Wathan pr	0	0	0	0
Leibrandt p	2	0	0	0
Quisenberry p	0	0	0	0
Iorg ph	1	0	1	2
Totals	32	2	10	2

St. Louis	0	0	0		0	0	0		0	1	0	–	1	5	0
Kansas City	0	0	0		0	0	0		0	0	2	–	2	10	0

St. Louis Cardinals	IP	H	R	ER	BB	SO
Cox	7.0	7	0	0	1	8
Dayley	1.0	0	0	0	1	2
Worrell L (0-1)	0.1	3	2	2	1	0
Totals	8.1	10	2	2	3	10

Kansas City Royals	IP	H	R	ER	BB	SO
Leibrandt	7.2	4	1	1	2	4
Quisenberry W (1-0)	1.1	1	0	0	0	1
Totals	9.0	5	1	1	2	5

E–None. DP–St. Louis 1, Kansas City 1. PB–Porter (1). 2B–Kansas City Smith (2,off Cox). SH–Leibrandt (2,off Cox). IBB–McRae (1,by Worrell). CS–White (1,2nd base by Cox/Porter). IBB–Worrell (1,McRae). U–Jim Quick (NL), Don Denkinger (AL), Bill Williams (NL), Jim McKean (AL), John Shulock (AL), Bob Engel (NL). T–2:47. A–41,628.

"An offensive team that can't bunt, handle the bat in key situations or run the bases will not be successful."

1985 World Series Box Scores

Game 7

Kansas City Royals 11, St. Louis Cardinals 0

At Royals Stadium

Game played on Sunday, October 27, 1985 at Royals Stadium

St. Louis Cardinals	ab	r	h	rbi	Kansas City Royals	ab	r	h	rbi
Smith ss	4	0	1	0	Smith lf	3	2	1	2
McGee cf	4	0	0	0	Jones lf	1	0	0	0
Herr 2b	4	0	0	0	Wilson cf	5	1	2	1
Clark 1b	4	0	1	0	Brett 3b	5	2	4	0
Van Slyke rf	4	0	1	0	White 2b	4	1	1	1
Pendleton 3b	3	0	1	0	Sundberg c	3	1	1	1
Landrum lf	2	0	1	0	Balboni 1b	4	2	2	2
Andujar p	0	0	0	0	Motley rf	4	1	3	3
Forsch p	0	0	0	0	Biancalana ss	3	0	0	0
Braun ph	1	0	0	0	Saberhagen p	4	1	0	0
Dayley p	0	0	0	0	Totals	36	11	14	10
Porter c	3	0	0	0					
Tudor p	1	0	0	0					
Campbell p	0	0	0	0					
Lahti p	0	0	0	0					
Horton p	0	0	0	0					
Jorgensen lf	2	0	0	0					
Totals	32	0	5	0					

St. Louis	0	0	0	0	0	0	0	0	0	–	0	5	0
Kansas City	0	2	3	0	6	0	0	0	x	–	11	14	0

St. Louis Cardinals	IP	H	R	ER	BB	SO
Tudor L (2-1)	2.1	3	5	5	4	1
Campbell	1.2	4	1	1	1	1
Lahti	0.2	4	4	4	0	1
Horton	0.0	1	1	1	0	0
Andujar	0.0	1	0	0	1	0
Forsch	1.1	1	0	0	0	1
Dayley	2.0	0	0	0	0	0
Totals	8.0	14	11	11	6	4

Kansas City Royals	IP	H	R	ER	BB	SO
Saberhagen W (2-0)	9.0	5	0	0	0	2
Totals	9.0	5	0	0	0	2

E–None. DP–St. Louis 2. 2B–Kansas City Smith (3,off Lahti). HR–Kansas City Motley (1,2nd inning off Tudor 1 on, 1 out). IBB–Biancalana (1,by Campbell). SB–Smith (2,3rd base off Tudor/Porter); Brett (1,2nd base off Tudor/Porter); Wilson (3,3rd base off Campbell/Porter). WP–Forsch (1). IBB–Campbell (1,Biancalana). U–Don Denkinger (AL), Bill Williams (NL), Jim McKean (AL), Bob Engel (NL), Jim Quick (NL), John Shulock (AL). T–2:46. A–41,658.

When I need to get away and relax, you'll see the GONE FISHING sign up on my door and I'm off with my friends or family members. It looks like this was a pretty good day fishing. That's something I used to do with my dad, and some of my fondest childhood memories are going of fishing with my dad and his friends. There's nothing as relaxing and peaceful, and peace and relaxation are two things that I could use right now. In this photo (l to r) Justin Randa, Bill Hillix, Gary Burgess and I do some striper fishing at Beaver Lake.

Acknowledgments:

Special Thanks to Bob Snodgrass, Bill Althaus, Cheryl Johnson, Lenny Cohen, Christine Drummond and Blake Hughes. Each of you spent numerous hours working hard, and I truly appreciate your hard work and dedication to this project.

My thanks and love to my sisters Mona, Joyce, Dianne, Erna and my older brother Vernon. It meant a lot to me knowing you were there for me throughout my career.

My brothers-in-law, Harvey A Williams Jr, Michael A. Williams, Dwayne A. Williams and Michael L. Craig, thanks for having my back. My sisters-in-law, Wanda Craig, Karen Williams, Sharon Hunt and Marilyn Williams, thank you for looking out for me. To the best mother-in-law ever Mary Williams, thanks for keeping everyone in line, I love you.

Thanks to the following people who have been there for me in many different ways - there are so many of you I apologize in advance if I forget to mention anyone: Sister Marie Neff, Earl and Linda Scroggins, Dick and Joanne Lacy, Jason and Deanna Deaton, Drew Dietrich, John Mayberry, Willie Wilson, Fred Patek, Greg Pryor, Jeff Montgomery, Brian McRae, Hal McRae, Amos Otis, U.L. Washington, Jim and Shirley Spaulding, Mamie Hughes, Chris Browne, Brian Watley, Paul Broome, Rich Hoffman, Mike Weber, Mike Carter, Mike Crawford, Bob Motley, Don Motley, Mark Eagleton and family, Mr. Earl Foster and family, Ralph A. Monaco II, Dan Sanders, Mickey Cobb, Nick Swartz, Aaron Racine, Dave Barber, Neil Harwell, John Dennison, Julia Irene Kaufman, John Wilson, Ronnie Johnson, Tommie Pannell, Bob Kendricks, Mayor Sly James, Don and Katie Byers, Kevin Shank, Steve and Erin Kurtenbach, T.J. Mcginnis, Ryan Lefebvre, Joel Goldberg, Kevin Keitzman, Chad Boeger, Richard Berkley, my pastor Rev. John Modest Miles, countless fans, friends and family, my heartfelt love and appreciation.

I want to also recognize and pay tribute to my friend Paul Splittorff, who made my transition to a baseball analyst a much easier transition than it would have been.

Last but certainly not least, my lovely wife Teresa. You are beautiful inside and out. Without your love and support it would have been impossible to get through everything that has happened the past year. We have shared so much, your kindness, support and loyalty is never ending. Thank you for being there for me no matter what the situation. I am truly blessed, lucky and smart to have married you. All my love.

-Frank White

A project like this has so many faces working feverishly behind the scenes, and they deserve some recognition. First and foremost, my mentor, friend and publisher Bob Snodgrass, who is a rock. Without his encouragement and patience, this project would have never become reality. He is a pro's pro and one of the best individuals I have ever worked with or called a friend. Jeff Barge, Tina Pearson and Nicole Calcara helped with the sometimes overwhelming job of transcription and Tim and Steve Pace gave me and Frank a quiet place to do interviews at Tim's Pizza in Independence. My wife Stacy basically spent a summer with her friends and by herself as Frank and I hammered out this autobiography and mere words cannot express how much I love her. (To Stacy: How have you put up with me the past 30 years?) And finally, I want to thank Frank. He spent more time with me this summer than he did his lovely wife Teresa. I've been involved in many projects with professional athletes and none have shown Frank's dedication. He was an amazing person to interview, a great editor and a man I have called a friend for more than 36 years. When he asked me to be a part of this project, I can say with complete honesty, that it was the greatest complement anyone has ever paid me. It took about half a second to say yes.

-Bill Althaus

Frank White

Frank White enjoyed a solid-gold career with the Kansas City Royals for 18 years. He became the premier second baseman of his era, winning a then record-tying eight Gold Gloves, earning five All-Star Game berths and hitting cleanup in the 1985 World Series, when the Royals came back from a 3-1 deficit to earn the team's lone world championship in seven games. White ended his career as a player in 1990 and in 1995, his No. 20 was retired by the team. That same year he was inducted into the Kansas City Royals Hall of Fame. He joined the Royals front office and later became a popular member of the Royals broadcasting team in 2008. He and his wife Teresa live in Lee's Summit, Missouri.

Bill Althaus

Bill Althaus is an award-winning sports writer and columnist for *The Examiner* in Eastern Jackson County. During the past three years the Missouri Press Association has honored him for his work at *The Examiner*. United Press International, the Associated Press and the Missouri Broadcasters Association have also recognized his work. He was named the Media Personality of the Year in 2006 by the Simone Award Committee, won the Morris Excellence in Journalism Award in 2007 and was named just the second winner of the Central Hockey League Media Service Award in 2010. Bill has written eight books. He lives with his wife Stacy in Grain Valley, Missouri.

Visit www.ascendbooks.com for more great titles
on your favorite teams and athletes.

www.ascendbooks.com